USBORNE
SOCCER SKILLS

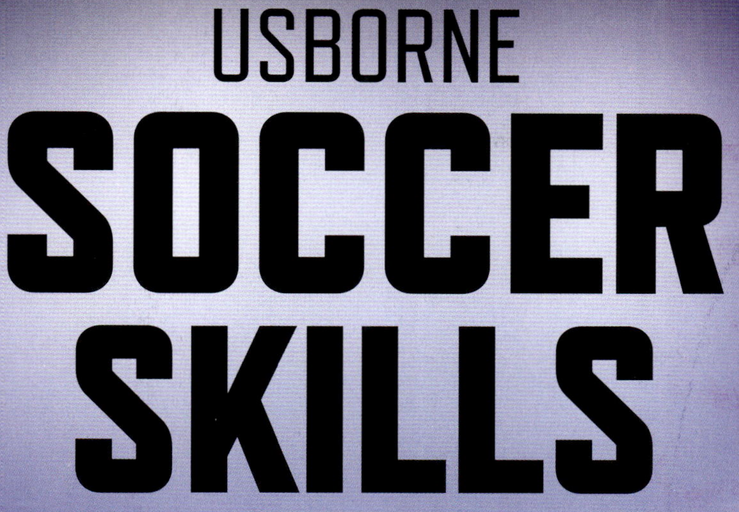

Katie Daynes and Simon Tudhope

Photography by
Alexandra Johnson
Illustrated by Fran Bueno
Designed by Krysia Ellis

With expert advice from
professional soccer player
Naomi Bedeau

American consultant: Mary Hearin,
Assistant Women's Soccer Coach,
University of Massachusetts

In association with
Show Racism the Red Card

CONTENTS

INTRO

Soccer is a game that everyone can play. All you need to get started is a ball. This book describes the main skills involved and suggests drills to help you practice them.

FOR EACH SKILL THERE'S A DIFFICULTY RATING OUT OF 10.

SOME OF THE DRILLS USE CONES OR A GOAL, BUT WATER BOTTLES AND SWEATSHIRTS CAN WORK JUST AS WELL.

USBORNE QUICKLINKS

For links to websites where you can watch video demonstrations of the skills in this book and pick up tips from professional players, go to **usborne.com/Quicklinks** and type in the book title.

Usborne Publishing is not responsible for the content or availability of external websites. Children should be supervised online. Please follow the internet safety guidelines at Usborne Quicklinks.

HOW TO HONE A SKILL

The best way to improve your game is to practice a skill again and again and again. That's what the pros do!

PRO TIP

Repeat a skill until it becomes so natural you don't need to think about it.

IN A GAME

Read the "in a game" suggestions to learn how different skills can be used on the field.

WHERE TO STRIKE

There are diagrams to show you how best to strike the ball.

FIRST TOUCH

Your first touch of the ball is crucial. You need to bring it under control quickly, so you're in charge of what happens next.

SKILL LEVEL

2 OUT OF **10**

PRO TIP

A good first touch makes it harder for your opponent to get the ball.

MOVE YOUR FOOT TO MEET THE BALL.

KEEP YOUR LEG RELAXED, SO THE BALL DOESN'T BOUNCE OFF YOUR FOOT.

CUSHION THE BALL WITH THE INSIDE OF YOUR FOOT.

IN A GAME

If the ball bounces off you, you could lose possession. But with it at your feet, you're in control.

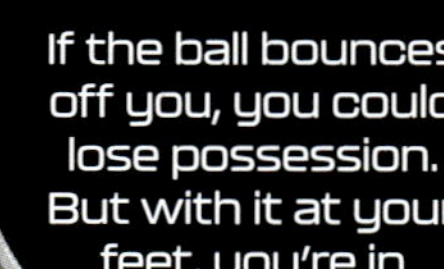

CUSHIONING THE BALL

Cushioning the ball means taking the speed out of it, just as a cushion would if it were attached to your body.

1 POSITION THE INSIDE OF YOUR FOOT IN LINE WITH THE ONCOMING BALL.

2 RELAX YOUR LEG AND LET YOUR FOOT TRAVEL BACK WITH THE BALL.

3 THE SPEED OF THE BALL IS ABSORBED. NOW YOU HAVE IT UNDER CONTROL.

TRAINING DRILL

With a teammate, practice cushioning the ball to improve your first touch.

Position two cones a short distance apart.

Play a diagonal pass to your teammate. They cushion the ball, play it onto their other foot, then pass back to you.

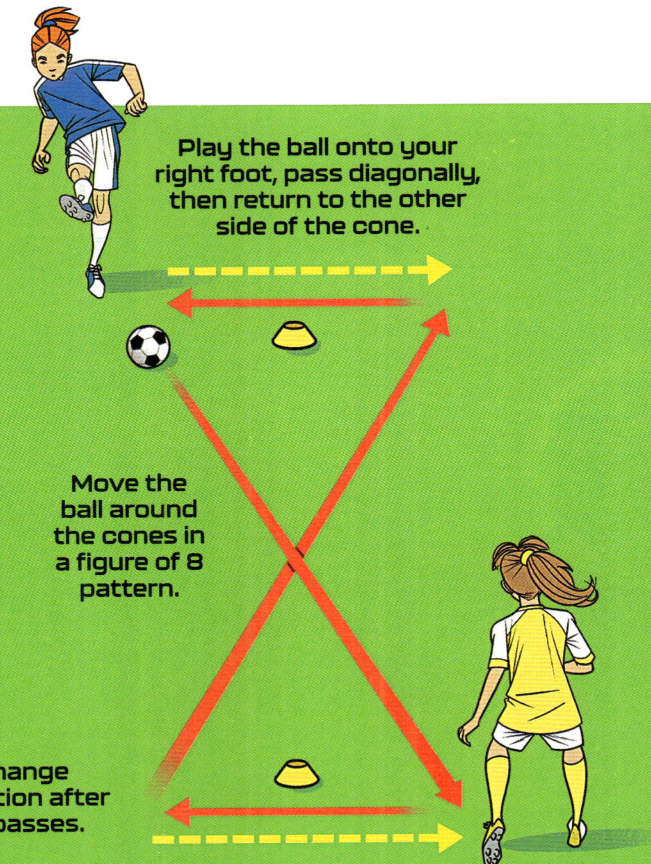

FOOT CONTROL

Often the ball will reach you in midair. To control it, you can use your foot to bring it down gently.

SKILL LEVEL 5 OUT OF 10

KEEP YOUR EYES ON THE BALL AS IT DROPS TOWARD YOUR FOOT.

GET YOUR WHOLE BODY BEHIND THE BALL.

RAISE YOUR FOOT SO THE LACES OF YOUR CLEAT MAKE CONTACT WITH THE BALL.

STIFFEN YOUR STANDING LEG.

PRO TIP

Core strength and balance drills will help you control the ball under pressure.

LOWER YOUR FOOT TO CUSHION THE BALL AS IT COMES DOWN.

HIGH BALL DRILLS

Practice controlling the ball as it drops toward you.

Start by throwing the ball straight up into the air and bringing your foot up to meet it as it falls.

Then work with a partner, taking turns to throw the ball.

The higher the ball, the harder it will be to control.

Use cones to mark out two squares, 3ft by 3ft (1m by 1m).

Stand in one square and throw the ball to your partner in the other square.

Lower your foot and try to control the ball inside your square.

Pass the ball back along the ground. Swap over when you've tried it five times.

DRILL VARIATION

If the ball is coming straight at you above waist height, you may need to use your chest to control it instead (see page 12).

JUGGLING

Juggling is great for improving your reactions, ball control and concentration.

SKILL LEVEL

7 OUT OF **10**

QUICKLINKS
Find useful juggling videos to help you get started.
usborne.com/Quicklinks

1 DRAG THE BALL BACK AND FLICK IT UP.

Flick gently so the ball stays close.

2 KEEP KICKING THE BALL UP WITHOUT LETTING IT TOUCH THE GROUND.

Use the top of your foot to control the ball.

PRO TIP
You can juggle anywhere - on the beach, in the yard, at the park...

3 TRY BOUNCING THE BALL OFF YOUR KNEE OR SHOULDER, TOO.

Can you manage a combination of moves?

HOW TO GET STARTED

Don't expect to be able to juggle a high number straight away. Here are three stages that can help you build up your skills.

1 DROP WITH BOUNCE

Drop the ball, let it bounce, then kick it up and catch it. Practice with both feet.

2 DROP NO BOUNCE

Drop the ball straight onto your foot, then kick it up and catch it. Practice with both feet.

3 DRAG BACK

Place your foot on top of the ball and roll it back.

Quickly move your foot under it...

...scoop it into the air and catch it.

SET A RECORD

Once you've mastered the technique, try keeping the ball up without catching it. How many kicks can you do before it touches the ground? Keep track, then try to beat your record!

CHEST CONTROL

SKILL LEVEL 6 OUT OF 10

Your chest is good for controlling awkward, high balls and bringing them safely to the ground.

HANDBALL!

It's a foul (against the rules) to deliberately touch the ball with any part of your arm below the shoulder, so keep both arms out of the way.

1 PUT YOUR ARMS BACK AND OPEN UP YOUR CHEST.

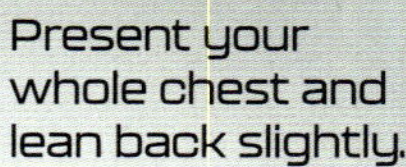

Present your whole chest and lean back slightly.

2 CUSHION THE BALL BY RELAXING AS IT MAKES CONTACT.

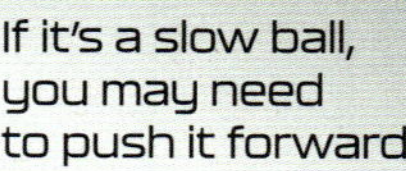

If it's a slow ball, you may need to push it forward.

3 BRING YOUR SHOULDERS IN SO THE BALL DROPS TO THE GROUND.

You want the ball to drop in front of you for your next touch.

CHEST DRILL

Do this drill in pairs to improve your chest control. Then you can use your chest in a game to set the ball up for a pass or shot.

YOUR PARTNER THROWS THE BALL SO IT LOOPS UP HIGH.

MOVE INTO POSITION TO RECEIVE THE BALL.

KEEP YOUR EYES ON THE BALL TO FOLLOW IT ONTO YOUR CHEST...

...THEN LET IT DROP TO THE GROUND AND PUSH PASS IT BACK.

SWAP OVER AFTER 10 THROWS.

DRILL PROGRESSION

Vary the angle, height and distance of the throws. Can you pass the ball back on your second touch?

PRO TIP

Keep your hands open, not clenched. It helps you stay relaxed.

DRIBBLING

One of the most exciting parts of soccer is running with the ball (dribbling). Learn to keep the ball under close control, even when you're running fast.

DRIBBLING DRILL

To dribble past your opponents, you'll often need to change direction. You can practice this by putting down cones and weaving between them.

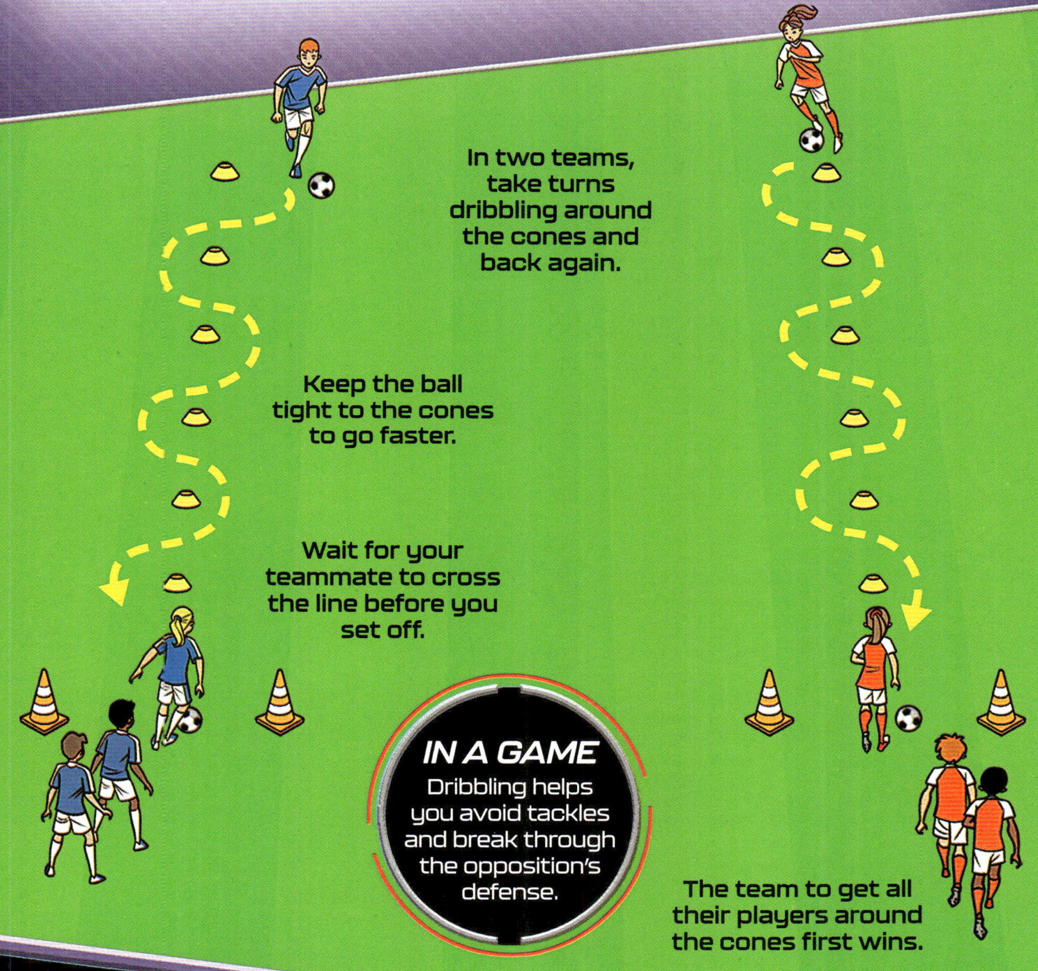

DRILL PROGRESSION

Try the same drill, but only making touches with your right foot, then only with your left foot. You can use both the inside and outside of your foot.

SHIELDING THE BALL

Shielding is a way of keeping possession of the ball. You use your body as a shield between the ball and your opponent.

USE YOUR ARM AND SHOULDER AS A BARRIER.

SKILL LEVEL

4 OUT OF 10

TURN YOUR BODY SO YOU'RE BETWEEN THE BALL AND THE OPPONENT.

THE OPPONENT RISKS COMMITTING A FOUL IF THEY TACKLE FROM BEHIND.

KEEP THE BALL CLOSE TO YOUR FEET.

USE YOUR STANDING FOOT TO GIVE YOU A STURDY BASE.

SHIELDING WHEN RUNNING

Watch out for opponents closing in on you, and be ready to change your body position to shield the ball.

PRO TIP

Lean into your opponent with your arm stretched out, to make a firm barrier.

IF AN OPPONENT COMES UP ON YOUR RIGHT, MOVE YOUR BODY TO THE RIGHT OF THE BALL.

IF AN OPPONENT COMES UP ON YOUR LEFT, MOVE YOUR BODY TO THE LEFT OF THE BALL.

IN A GAME

If the ball comes off your opponent and is going out of play, shield it so they can't keep it in.

FEINTING

Feinting means tricking your opponent by pretending to go one way, then going the other.

SELLING A FAKE

Feinting is also known as "selling a fake."
You need to be confident and convincing
in your movement for it to work.
Practice the steps below in pairs.

1 PRETEND TO MOVE IN ONE DIRECTION WITH THE BALL SO YOUR PARTNER DOES THE SAME.

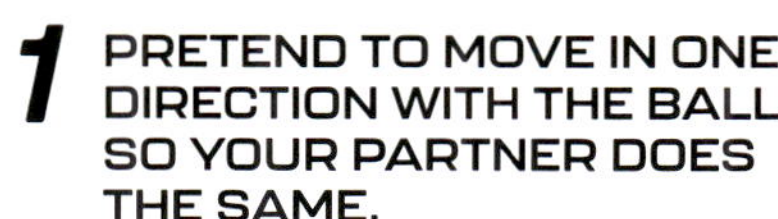

2 QUICKLY SHIFT YOUR WEIGHT AND TAKE THE BALL IN THE OTHER DIRECTION.

IN A GAME

Use feinting when you're one-on-one with the goalkeeper, to send them the wrong way.

PRO TIP

If you're the defender, watch the ball not the player, so you're not fooled.

3 SLIP PAST YOUR PARTNER, THEN SWAP ROLES.

TRICK TURNS

If you're being closely marked, a trick turn is a great way to lose your opponent. There are several different kinds of turns. Here's how to do a drag-back turn.

QUICKLINKS
Discover more trick turns, including scissors, stepovers and drag-backs.
usborne.com/Quicklinks

1 PRETEND TO KICK THE BALL, BUT PLACE YOUR FOOT ON TOP OF IT INSTEAD.

2 DRAG THE BALL BACK BEHIND YOU.

3 SPIN ON YOUR OTHER FOOT AND LEAN TOWARD THE BALL.

4 COMPLETE THE TURN AND ACCELERATE AWAY.

THE CRUYFF TURN

This turn was named after the great Dutch player Johan Cruyff. It's a neat way to turn 180 degrees on the spot.

1 SHAPE YOUR BODY AS IF YOU'RE ABOUT TO KICK THE BALL.

2 SWING YOUR LEG PAST THE BALL, THEN PULL IT BACK WITH THE INSIDE OF YOUR FOOT.

3 SWIVEL AROUND AND ACCELERATE AWAY.

HEEL TRICKS

SKILL LEVEL 9 OUT OF 10

Heel tricks are rarely used in games, but they're fun to try and will improve your ball control, too.

THE RAINBOW FLICK

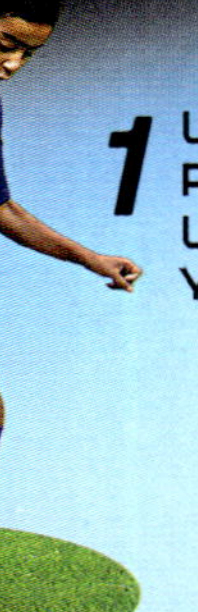

1 USE ONE FOOT TO ROLL THE BALL UP THE INSIDE OF YOUR OTHER LEG.

2 THEN FLICK IT UP AND OVER YOUR HEAD WITH THE OTHER HEEL.

QUICKLINKS
Watch videos of impressive heel tricks in action, including the rainbow flick.
usborne.com/Quicklinks

3 RUN FORWARD TO MEET THE BALL AS IT LANDS.

THE HEEL CATCH

1 WHILE THE BALL IS IN THE AIR, MOVE IN FRONT OF IT AND LEAN FORWARD.

2 BEND YOUR LEG AND CATCH THE BALL BETWEEN YOUR HEEL AND YOUR BOTTOM.

PRO TIP

You can move from juggling to a heel catch by kicking the ball up high.

3 TO RELEASE THE BALL, SWING YOUR LEG FORWARD.

4 CAN YOU KEEP THE BALL IN THE AIR BY ADDING SOME JUGGLES?

Heel tricks are great freestyle moves. Turn the page to find out more about freestyle soccer, and learn some extra tricks.

FREESTYLE TRICKS

Freestyle soccer is the art of juggling a soccer ball using fancy flicks and tricks to show off your control.

SKILL LEVEL

9 OUT OF **10**

"AROUND THE WORLD" IS A GOOD TRICK TO PRACTICE.

FLICK THE BALL UP AND MOVE YOUR FOOT AROUND IT IN A COMPLETE CIRCLE.

THEN FLICK THE BALL UP AGAIN WITH THE SAME FOOT BEFORE IT TOUCHES THE GROUND.

QUICKLINKS
Watch freestylers perform an amazing range of soccer skills and tricks.
usborne.com/Quicklinks

FIND YOUR OWN STYLE

There's no limit to the tricks and combinations you can try. Freestyle soccer is a sport in itself, with competitions all over the world.

EXPERIMENT WITH DIFFERENT MOVES. IT'S GREAT FOR IMPROVING BALANCE AND CONTROL.

SITTING TRICKS ARE KNOWN AS SIT-DOWNS. PUT YOUR HANDS ON THE GROUND FOR SUPPORT.

PUSH PASS

SKILL LEVEL 2 OUT OF 10

This is a kick along the ground to a nearby teammate. It's accurate and easy to learn.

WHERE TO STRIKE

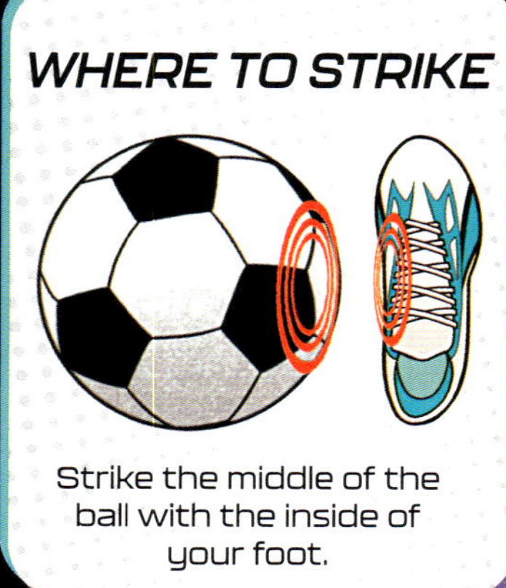

Strike the middle of the ball with the inside of your foot.

YOUR KICKING FOOT IS ALMOST AT A RIGHT ANGLE TO YOUR OTHER FOOT.

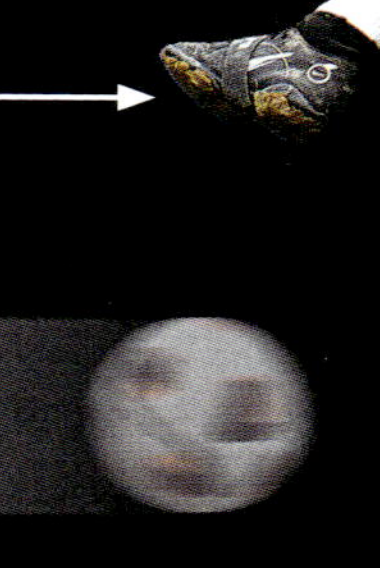

1 PLACE ONE FOOT BY THE BALL AND LIFT YOUR OTHER FOOT BACK.

2 KEEP YOUR EYE ON THE BALL AS YOU SWING YOUR FOOT FORWARD.

3 STRIKE FIRMLY WITH THE INSIDE OF YOUR FOOT.

Hold your body fairly straight.

Stiffen your ankle when you make contact.

Follow through smoothly.

PASSING DRILL

Work in pairs and place two markers 2ft (60cm) apart. Stand either side of the markers and pass to each other through the gap. Score a point for each successful pass.

PRO TIP

Strike the ball firmly, so the pass is harder to intercept.

DRILL PROGRESSION

After five passes each, move another 3ft (1m) apart and start again. Carry on until you are 30ft (10m) apart. The player with the most points wins.

ONE-TWO

A one-two involves two quick passes between you and a teammate. It's a useful way to beat the defense and move the ball at speed.

WHEN YOUR PATH IS BLOCKED BY A DEFENDER, QUICKLY PASS TO A TEAMMATE.

YOU CAN THEN DASH PAST THE DEFENDER...

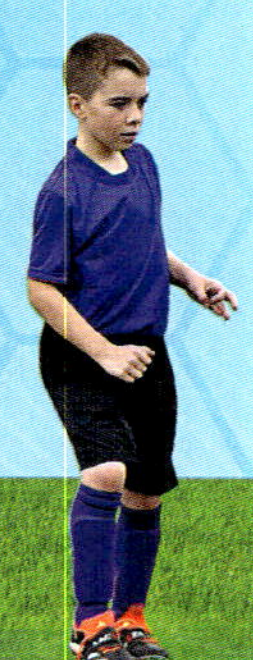

...AND RECEIVE THE RETURN PASS WITH MORE SPACE AHEAD OF YOU.

ONE-TWO DRILL

Mark out an area 80 x 20ft (24 x 6m). The player with the ball has to get past four defenders, using a mixture of one-two passes and dribbling.

The defenders make a line down the center.

FINISH

The attackers stand at the sides.

START

Run toward each defender, and either pass or dribble around them. Keep the defender guessing!

Swap with a teammate once you've lost the ball or reached the end.

Score a point for each defender you get past. Who can get the furthest?

CROSSING

A cross is a long sideways pass into the box (penalty area). If you're attacking down the wing, it's a great way to set up a goal.

SKILL LEVEL

7 OUT OF **10**

SWING YOUR LEG ACROSS YOUR BODY AND THROUGH THE BALL.

HOLD YOUR ARMS OUT TO IMPROVE YOUR BALANCE.

IN A GAME

The penalty spot is a good place to aim for to give your forwards a chance to score.

WRAP YOUR FOOT AROUND THE OUTSIDE OF THE BALL SO IT CURLS IN.

A SIMILAR TECHNIQUE CAN BE USED FOR A CORNER KICK. FIND OUT MORE ON PAGE 68.

CROSS DRILL

Work on your crossing skills in a group of three. Player A passes to player B, who dribbles down the wing, then crosses the ball to player C.

DRILL PROGRESSION

Add in a player to defend the cross, so you have to curl the ball over them.

LOW INSTEP DRIVE

Your instep is the top part of your foot where your laces are. If you want to kick the ball a long way, take a run-up and use your instep.

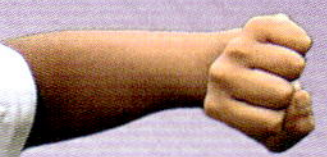

PRO TIP

The secret to making the kick accurate is to hit the ball straight through the middle.

PASSING DRILL

Try this drill for four players, to help develop your instep kicking technique.

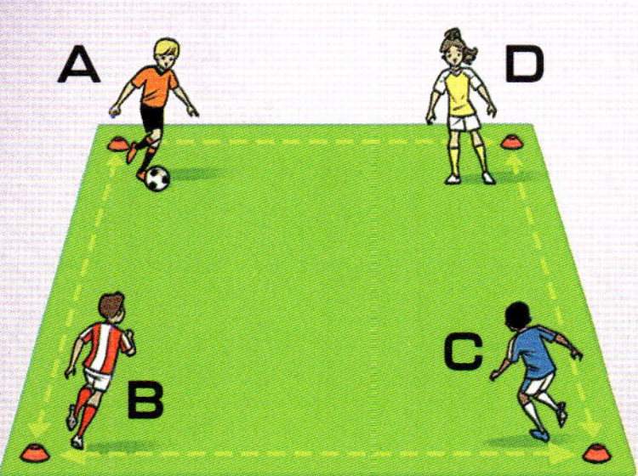

Mark out a 90ft (30m) square. The four players start in each corner.

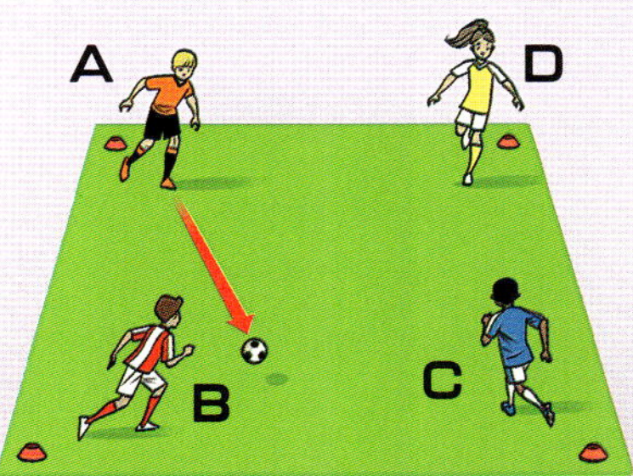

Player A passes the ball in front of B. B runs onto it and passes in front of C.

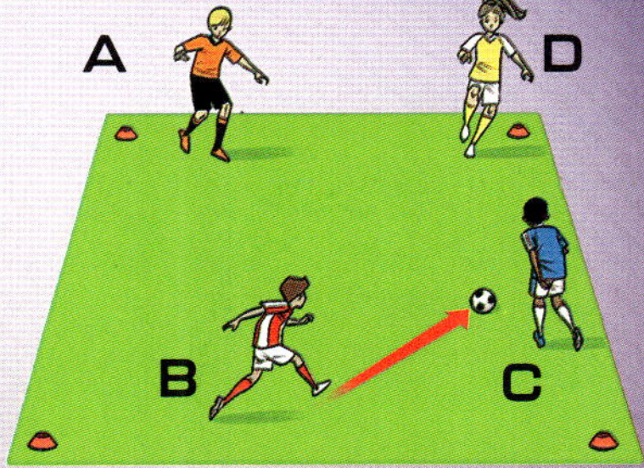

C passes to D, D to A... and the game continues around the square.

DON'T LEAN BACK, AND KEEP YOUR TOES POINTED DOWN...

...SO THE BALL STAYS LOW.

IN A GAME

The low instep drive is great for long-range passes. They're fast and direct, so hard to intercept.

WHERE TO STRIKE

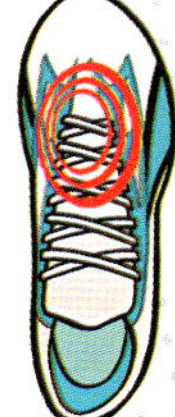

Strike the ball through the middle with your instep (where your laces are).

LOFTED PASS

The lofted pass is a long, high kick. The technique is similar to the low instep drive, but you need to get under the ball more.

1 RUN AT THE BALL, SWING YOUR LEG BACK AND LOOK DOWN.

2 MAKE CONTACT WITH THE LOWER HALF OF THE BALL.

3 SWING YOUR FOOT UP IN ONE SMOOTH MOTION.

Your instep should reach under the ball.

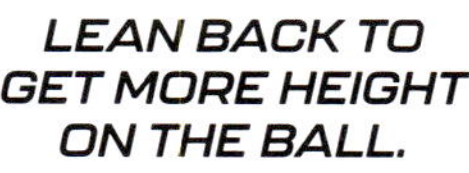

LEAN BACK TO GET MORE HEIGHT ON THE BALL.

Kick the lower half of the ball to make it rise.

LOFTED PASS PRACTICE

Lofted passes need to be accurate as well as powerful to reach their target. You can practice by trying to pass the ball over one or two other players.

Mark out a row of four boxes, all 30ft (10m) square. One player stands in each box.

A and D try to lob the ball over B and C. They score a point for each successful pass.

If B or C manage to intercept the ball, they take the places of A and D, and start scoring points for their own successful passes.

INSIDE FOOT SWERVE

Swerving or bending the ball can be really useful when passing or shooting. It's easiest to make the ball swerve using the inside of your foot.

SKILL LEVEL 7 OUT OF 10

1 PLANT YOUR NON-KICKING FOOT BESIDE THE BALL.

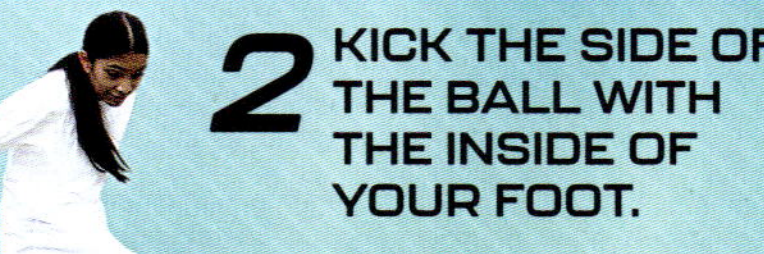

2 KICK THE SIDE OF THE BALL WITH THE INSIDE OF YOUR FOOT.

3 LET YOUR FOOT FOLLOW THROUGH IN LINE WITH THE CURVE.

THE BALL SHOULD KEEP FAIRLY LOW AND SWERVE INWARD.

WHERE TO STRIKE

Kick the ball low down with the inside of your foot.

SWERVE DRILL

Practice swerving the ball by placing two cones 2ft (60cm) apart and trying to pass the ball around them. You could try this in a group of three.

Two players stand 30ft (10m) apart. The third player stands halfway between them.

The player in the middle tries to intercept the ball, but can't move outside the cones.

If the ball is intercepted or goes too wide, the player who kicked it swaps into the middle.

How many times can you pass the ball before it's intercepted?

Practice swerving the ball one way with your left leg and the other way with your right leg.

DRILL PROGRESSION

Widen the cone area and add another player in the middle. Now you have to bend the ball even more.

OUTSIDE FOOT SWERVE

SKILL LEVEL 9 OUT OF 10

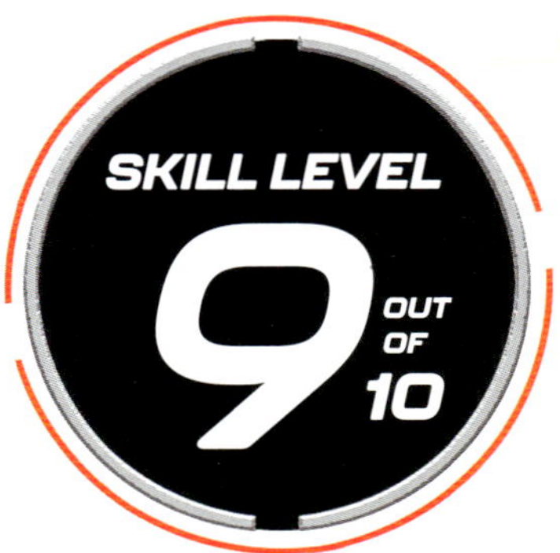

This kick makes the ball swerve the opposite way to an inside foot swerve. It's tricky to master, but very useful.

1 SWING YOUR LEG BACK AND ANGLE YOUR FOOT IN.

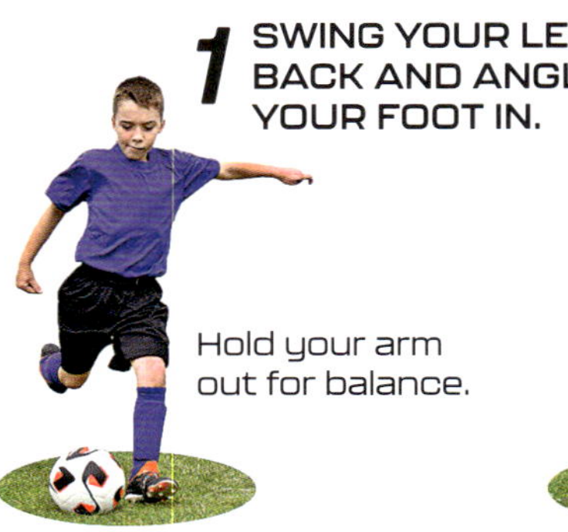

Hold your arm out for balance.

2 MAKE CONTACT WITH THE OUTSIDE OF YOUR FOOT.

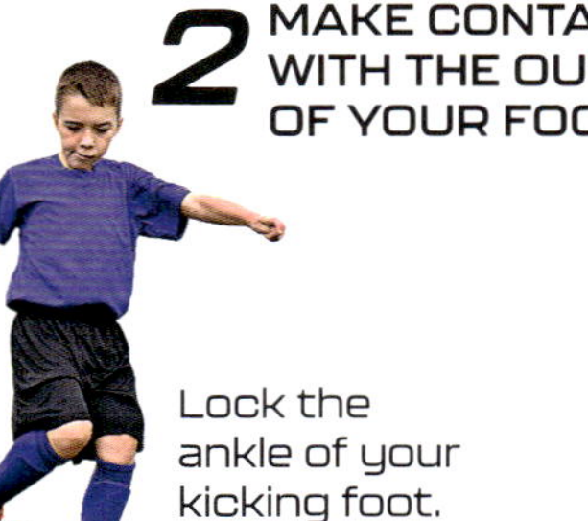

Lock the ankle of your kicking foot.

3 USE PLENTY OF FOLLOW-THROUGH.

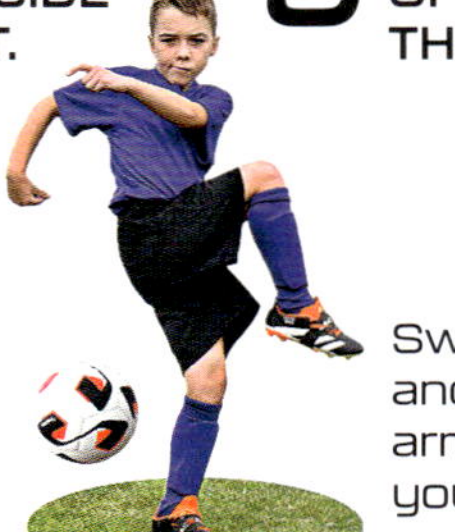

Sweep your leg and opposite arm across your body.

QUICKLINKS
Watch training videos with tips on how to kick inside and outside foot swerves.
usborne.com/Quicklinks

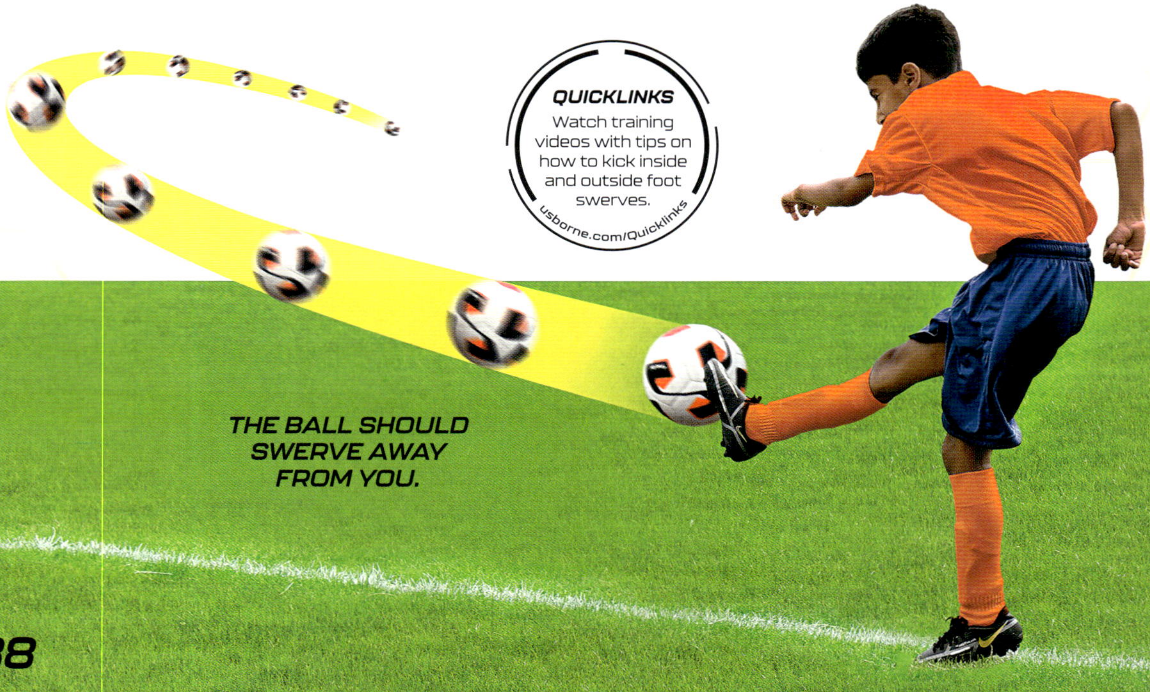

THE BALL SHOULD SWERVE AWAY FROM YOU.

PAIRS PRACTICE

Pass the ball to your teammate using an outside swerve. Place a marker halfway between you, and try to make the ball swerve around it.

Control the ball then swerve it back to your partner.

WHERE TO STRIKE

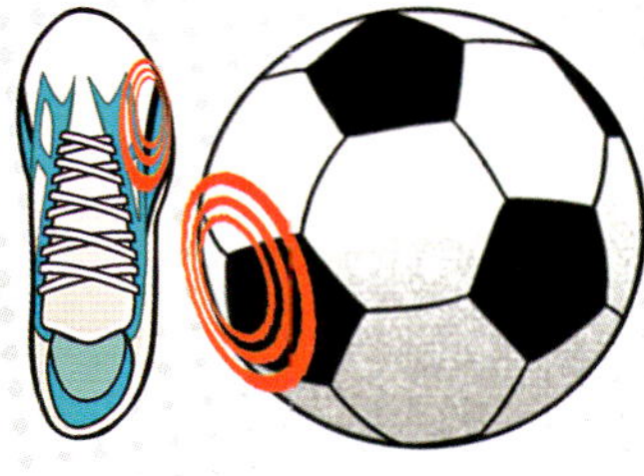

Angle your foot down and strike the side of the ball with the area by your little toe.

Practice with both your right and left foot, sending the ball either side of the cone.

DRILL PROGRESSION

Try to make the ball go higher by kicking through its lower half, with your foot at less of an angle. This becomes a lofted swerve kick.

SKILL LEVEL

6 OUT OF 10

FRONT VOLLEY

A volley is when you kick the ball while it's in the air. You need quick reactions and good accuracy.

WHEN VOLLEYING AT GOAL, KEEP YOUR HEAD OVER THE BALL OR YOU'LL BALLOON IT OVER THE BAR.

1 SWING YOUR LEG BACK AND POINT YOUR TOES DOWN.

2 KICK THROUGH THE LOWER HALF OF THE BALL.

3 FOLLOW THROUGH WITH YOUR TOES STILL POINTED.

You can also volley with the side of your foot.

LEARNING TO VOLLEY

Work with a friend. Stand 10ft (3m) apart. Drop the ball onto your foot and volley it for them to catch.

DRILL PROGRESSION

Rather than dropping the ball, get your partner to throw it to you and volley it back into their hands.

SIDE VOLLEY

To do a side volley, you need to balance on one leg while leaning sideways, then swing your leg around.

SKILL LEVEL

9 OUT OF **10**

1 LEAN AWAY FROM THE BALL.

Have your arms up for balance.

2 SWING YOUR LEG AROUND TO THE SIDE.

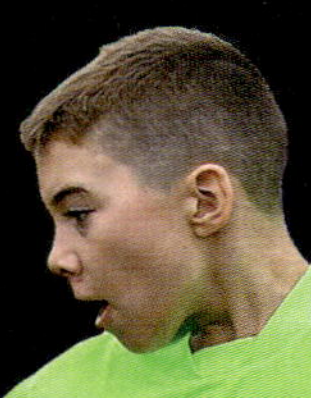

Strike the ball with your instep.

PRO TIP

Point your non-kicking foot in the direction you want the ball to go in.

3 FOLLOW THROUGH BY SWINGING YOUR LEG ACROSS YOUR BODY.

VOLLEY DRILL

Find something that's almost as high as your hip, and try swinging your leg over it.

Once you've got a smooth action, try putting the ball on top and side-volleying it.

DRILL PROGRESSION

Practice in a group of three, taking turns to throw, volley or catch the ball. Score a point for each accurate volley.

IN A GAME

Goalies can throw the ball up and side-volley it for a fast, flat goal kick.

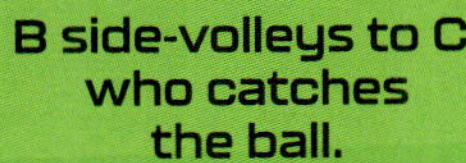

CHIPPING

The chip is a precise little kick that gets the ball quickly up and down. It's ideal for lifting the ball over the goalkeeper.

SKILL LEVEL

5 OUT OF **10**

1 FACE THE BALL STRAIGHT ON AND TAKE A SHORT BACKSWING.

2 BRING YOUR FOOT DOWN WITH A SHARP STABBING ACTION.

3 YOUR FOOT KICKS INTO THE GROUND AS IT HITS THE BALL.

QUICKLINKS

See some of the best chip shots made by professional players.

usborne.com/Quicklinks

THERE'S NO FOLLOW THROUGH WITH A CHIP, SINCE YOUR FOOT HITS THE GROUND.

CHIPPING DRILL

To practice chipping, you need someone to roll or kick the ball to you. See if you can chip it back over their head.

Then try this exercise in a group of three, taking turns to chip the ball over the middle player.

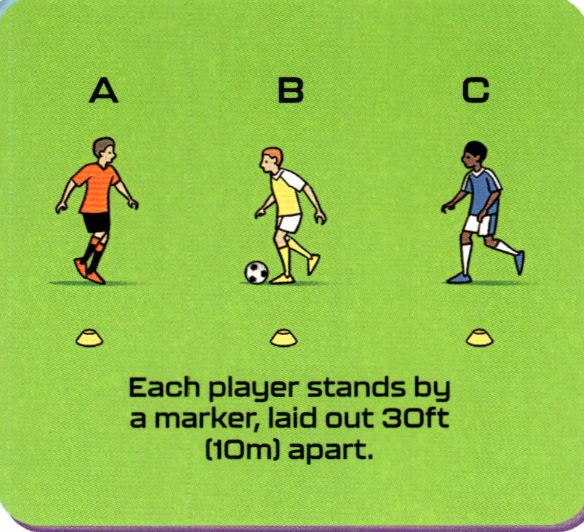

Each player stands by a marker, laid out 30ft (10m) apart.

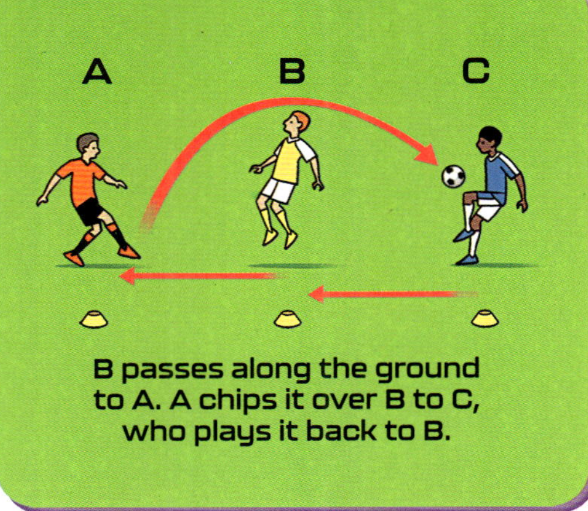

B passes along the ground to A. A chips it over B to C, who plays it back to B.

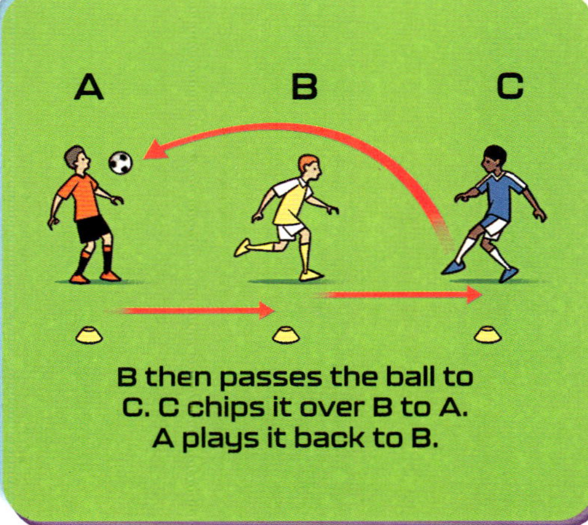

B then passes the ball to C. C chips it over B to A. A plays it back to B.

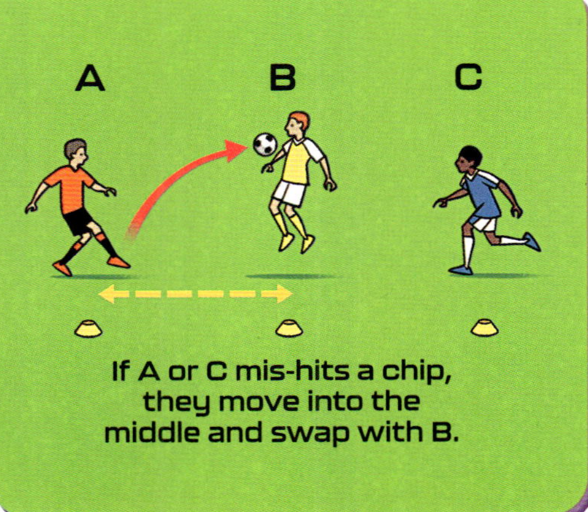

If A or C mis-hits a chip, they move into the middle and swap with B.

PLACING A SHOT

To give yourself the best chance of scoring, it's important to learn how to place your shot just where you want it.

SKILL LEVEL

6 OUT OF **10**

QUICKLINKS
Discover core skills to master for striking the ball with accuracy.
usborne.com/Quicklinks

PLACE YOUR SHOT WITH THE SIDE OF YOUR FOOT.

ACCURACY IS MORE IMPORTANT THAN POWER.

AIM JUST INSIDE THE GOAL POST.

BE READY FOR A REBOUND OFF THE GOALIE OR THE POST.

TRY TO SHOOT LOW OVER THE GROUND OR HIGH INTO THE ROOF OF THE NET.

TARGET PRACTICE

You can improve your aim by marking a target on a wall to shoot at, but it's even better to practice against a goalkeeper.

PRO TIP
To improve accuracy, let your leg follow through toward the target.

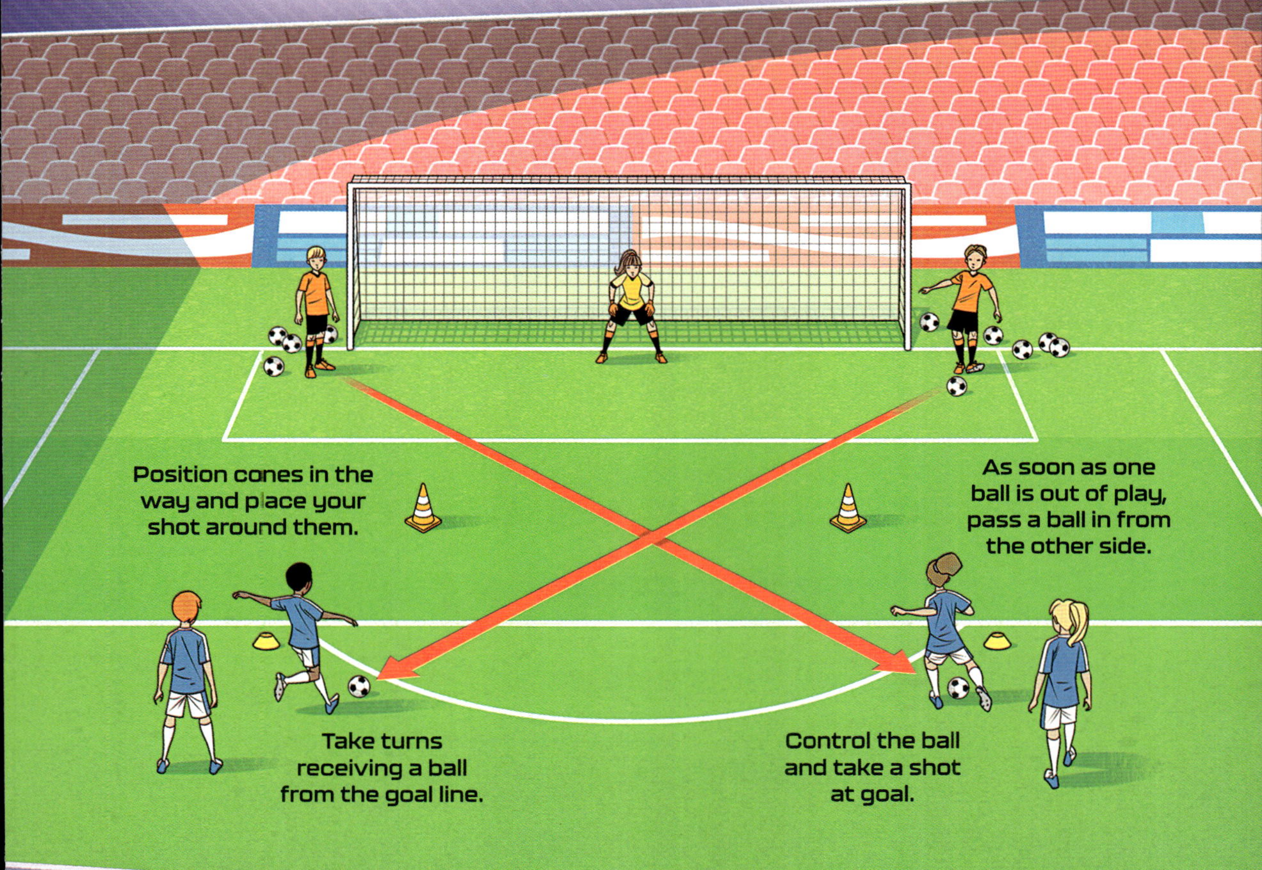

DRILL PROGRESSION

Replace the cones with players who will close you down as you aim to shoot. This is good practice for getting your shot off quickly.

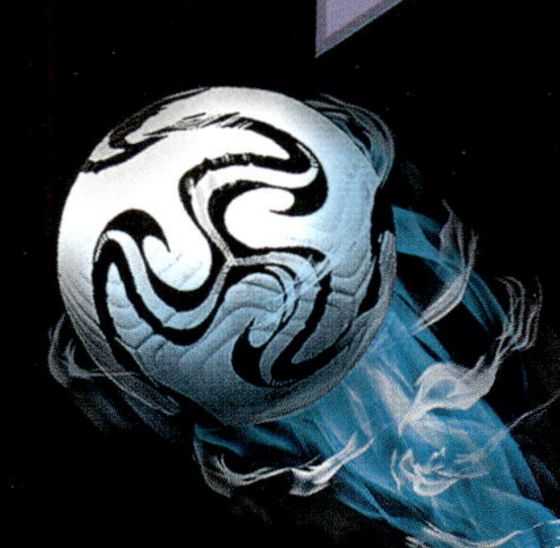

STRIKING THE BALL

For a powerful shot, use an instep drive to strike the ball firmly and cleanly. This is also known as lacing the ball.

PRO TIP

Aim for the top corner of the goal and keep your hips facing your target.

SKILL LEVEL

7 OUT OF **10**

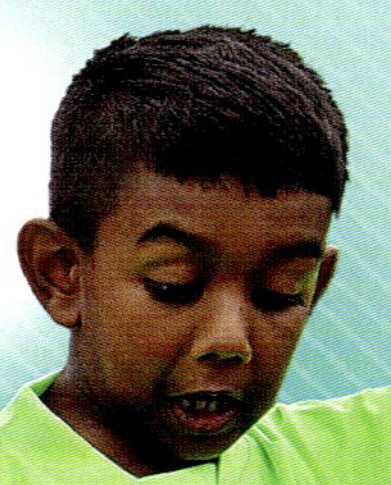

KEEP YOUR HEAD OVER THE BALL AND YOUR EYES DOWN AS YOU KICK.

Strike through the middle of the ball to keep it under the bar.

POINT YOUR TOES DOWN, SO YOU MAKE CONTACT WITH YOUR INSTEP.

PLANT YOUR NON-KICKING FOOT NEXT TO THE BALL.

STRIKE DRILLS

First, practice your technique on a stationary ball. You could aim at a rebound fence, so the ball doesn't go too far.

Place your ball a short distance from the fence. Take a short run up... and strike it hard.

Next, try this drill with a moving ball. A player passes the ball to you in front of goal and you have three touches to score.

1 CONTROL THE BALL.   **2** TOUCH IT FORWARD.   **3** STRIKE!

BEATING THE GOALIE

The goalkeeper will often rush out to block your shot. Here are some options for what to do next.

SKILL LEVEL
6 OUT OF 10

CHIPPING

Try chipping the ball over the goalie. It takes a delicate touch to get the ball up and down into the goal.

DRIBBLING

Try dribbling around the goalkeeper by feinting one way then darting the other.

KEEP YOUR EYES ON BOTH THE BALL AND THE GOALIE'S POSITION.

THE GOALIE HAS TO TIME THEIR DIVE JUST RIGHT, OR THEY MIGHT GIVE AWAY A PENALTY.

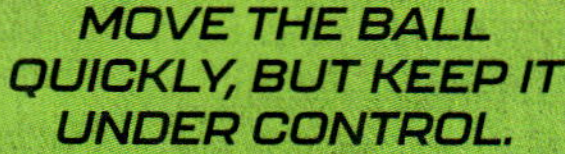

MOVE THE BALL QUICKLY, BUT KEEP IT UNDER CONTROL.

JOCKEYING

Jockeying means delaying your opponent's attack by getting in their way. Keep your body between them and the goal, and try to force them in a different direction.

SKILL LEVEL

5 OUT OF **10**

IN A GAME
Jockeying keeps your opponent away from your goal.

KEEP YOUR EYES ON THE BALL, NOT THE PLAYER.

MAKE YOUR BODY AN OBSTACLE IN THEIR WAY.

PRO TIP
Don't rush in toward your opponent too quickly, or they'll dodge past you.

GOAL

KEEP YOUR WEIGHT ON YOUR KNEES, SO YOU'RE IN A STRONG POSITION TO CHALLENGE.

MAINTAINING PRESSURE

Practice jockeying in pairs. Try to force the other player away from goal or onto their weaker side. If they use their right foot, they're likely to be weaker on their left – and vice versa.

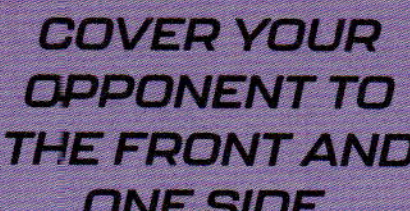

COVER YOUR OPPONENT TO THE FRONT AND ONE SIDE.

Jockeying on this attacker's right forces them to the left.

KEEP JOCKEYING TO FORCE THEM AWAY FROM GOAL.

The attacker is being forced toward the touchline (sideline).

ONCE YOU HAVE YOUR OPPONENT UNDER PRESSURE, WATCH FOR OPPORTUNITIES TO WIN THE BALL.

The defender blocks the ball out for a throw-in.

INTERCEPTING

The most direct way to win the ball is by tackling your opponent, but if you can intercept the ball instead, it's easier to keep possession.

WHEN TO INTERCEPT

Sometimes it's better to stay between the attacker and the goal rather than trying a risky interception – because if you miss the ball, you may leave them with a clear run on goal.

INTERCEPTING DRILL

Try this drill for three players. One player passes to another, and the third decides whether or not to intercept.

Start by marking out a 30ft (10m) square with four cones.

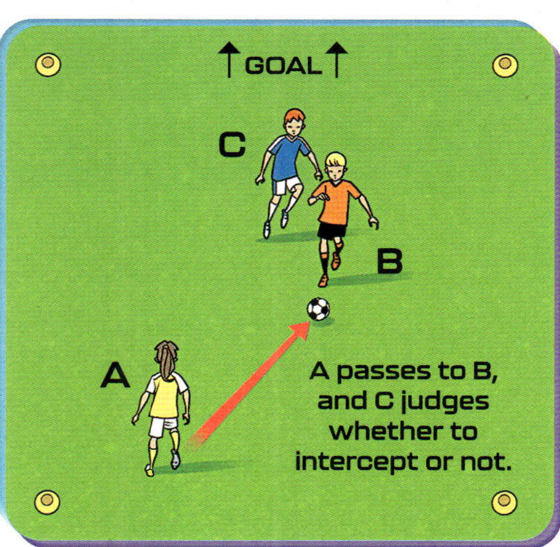

OPTION 1
C decides not to intercept.

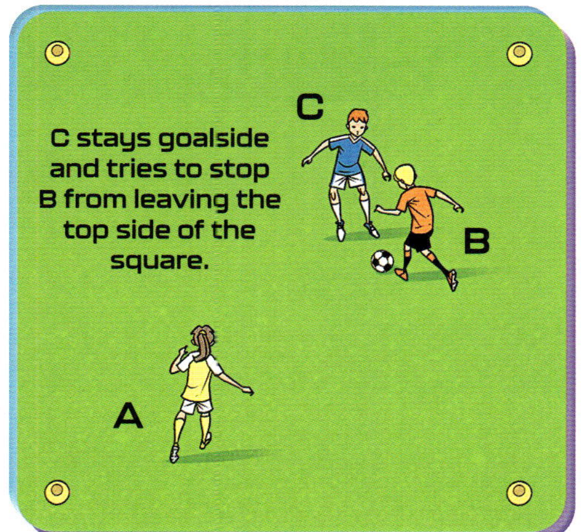

C stays goalside and tries to stop B from leaving the top side of the square.

OPTION 2
C decides to intercept.

If C manages to get the ball, they then pass back to A.

BLOCK TACKLE

To win the ball off your opponent, your tackling needs to be hard but fair. It requires good timing and a clear head. If you miss the ball or barge into the other player, you might give away a foul.

MOVE FORWARD SO YOU HAVE THE WEIGHT OF YOUR WHOLE BODY BEHIND THE TACKLE.

FOOT POSITION

Use the inside of your tackling foot.

MAKE CONTACT WITH THE MIDDLE OF THE BALL...

...AND FORCE IT AWAY FROM THE OTHER PLAYER.

TACKLE DRILL

In pairs, mark out a 30ft (10m) line. One player has the ball while the other player tries to tackle.

TACKLING ANGLES

Use a block tackle to challenge from the front or the side.

IN A GAME

Block tackles are useful in a crowded situation, or when there's a lcose ball and two players have an equal chance of winning it.

SLIDE TACKLE

If you're not in the right position for a block tackle, you might need to make a slide tackle to stop a dangerous attack.

FOUL!

It's a foul to lunge with both feet or to tackle with your studs up. The referee will award a free kick and may give you a yellow or red card (see page 96).

KEEP IT CLEAN

Here are some tips to avoid fouling in a slide tackle.

- Be patient and wait for the right moment.
- Keep your non-tackling leg tucked underneath you, so you never slide in with both legs.
- Make contact with the ball.

It's best to practice slide tackles with a cone instead of an opponent, so you're less likely to hurt someone.

PRACTICE SLIDING WITH EITHER LEG.

THE AIM IS TO SLIDE THE BALL AWAY, WITHOUT TOUCHING THE CONE.

TAKE A FAST RUN UP AND REALLY GO FOR IT.

You could practice your slide tackle timing in pairs.

Your partner passes the ball to the side of your cone.

You then have to time your slide to make contact with the ball but not the cone.

FORMING A WALL

If a free kick is given in shooting range, players line up to make a defensive "wall." The wall covers one side of the goal, while the goalkeeper covers the other side.

THE TALLEST PLAYER STANDS IN LINE WITH THE POST FURTHEST FROM THE GOALIE.

FORM THE WALL QUICKLY.

JUMP AS THE BALL COMES TOWARD YOU.

STAND CLOSE, LEAVING NO GAPS.

ONE PLAYER CAN LIE DOWN TO STOP ANY LOW SHOTS UNDER THE WALL.

BE READY TO BLOCK ANY REBOUNDS.

POSITIONING THE WALL

For central kicks, the goal is more open so you need more defenders in the wall.

For kicks from the side, there's less of the goal to aim at. The striker is more likely to pass the ball than take a shot.

TEAM COMMUNICATION

If you don't communicate well during a game, you'll end up losing the ball. Using some standard calls will help you work as a team and avoid confusion.

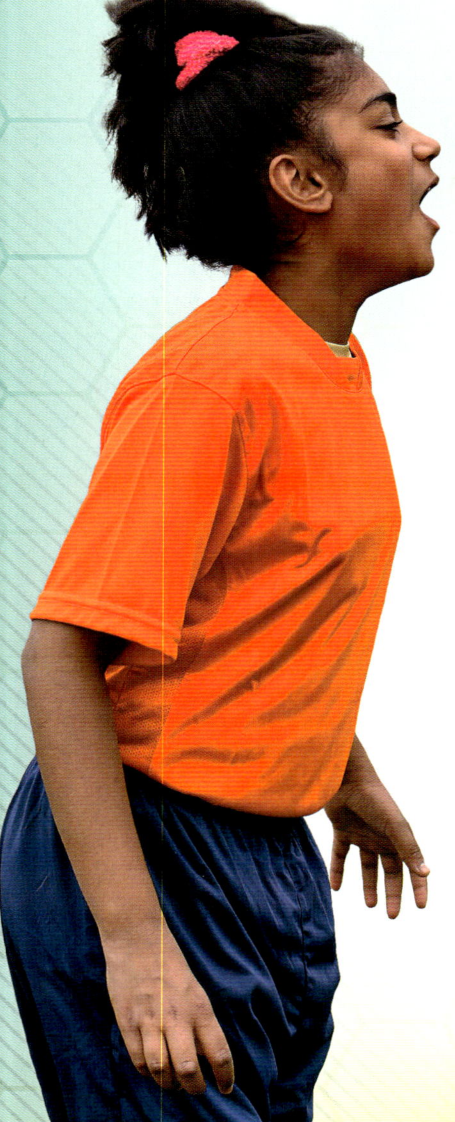

TANAYA'S BALL!
Shouting your name tells your teammates to leave the ball for you.

TIME!
This tells a teammate they're unmarked and can take their time.

PLAYER-ON!
This warns a teammate that an opponent is approaching.

FORCE THEM OUTSIDE!
This tells defenders to force an attacker away from the goal.

COMMUNICATION DRILL

Try this drill to practice your communication skills. Players use calls to help them attack and defend.

The players have to keep the ball within a 30ft x 60ft (10m x 20m) box.

Two defenders try to intercept the ball or make a tackle.

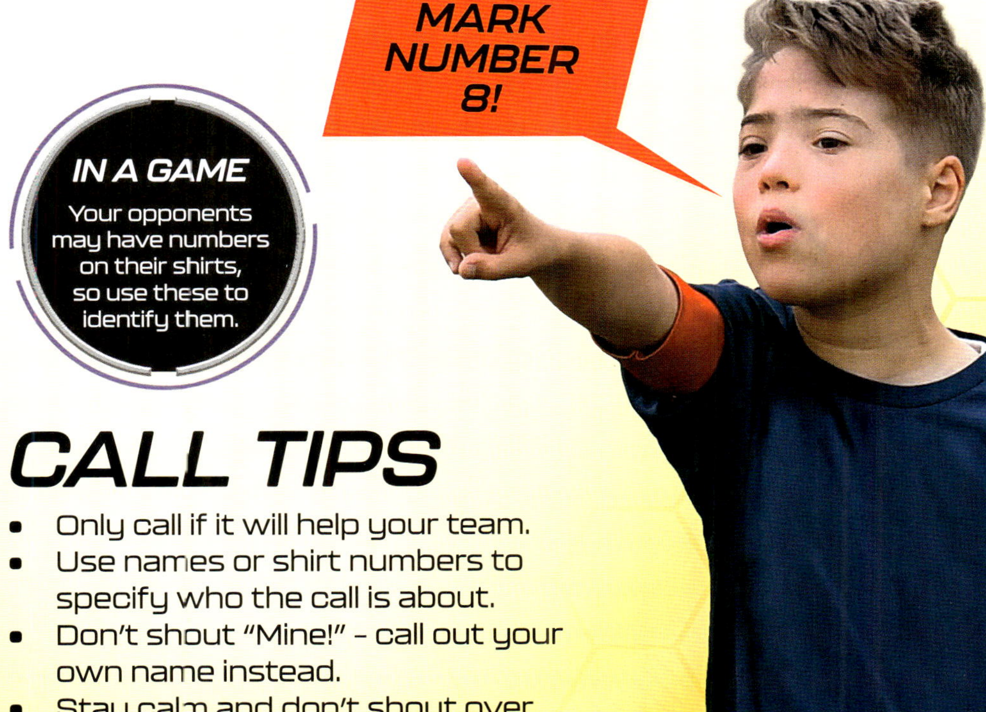

CALL TIPS

- Only call if it will help your team.
- Use names or shirt numbers to specify who the call is about.
- Don't shout "Mine!" – call out your own name instead.
- Stay calm and don't shout over each other.

THROW-IN TECHNIQUE

When the ball goes over the touchline (the line at the side of the field), the team that touched it last loses possession, and the other team gets to throw it back in.

THROW THE BALL FROM BEHIND YOUR HEAD WITH BOTH HANDS.

TAKE THE THROW-IN FROM THE PLACE WHERE THE BALL WENT OUT.

THE THROWER CAN'T TOUCH THE BALL AGAIN UNTIL AFTER ANOTHER PLAYER HAS TOUCHED IT.

FOUL THROW?

Follow the throw-in rules carefully, or the ref will blow for a foul throw (see page 67). And don't throw the ball straight into the goal – that's a foul too!

MAKE SURE YOUR FEET AREN'T OVER THE LINE.

KEEP BOTH FEET ON THE GROUND WHEN YOU THROW.

PRACTICING THROW-INS

Stand about 30ft (10m) apart and practice throwing the ball to your teammate's feet. Remember to release it from behind your head.

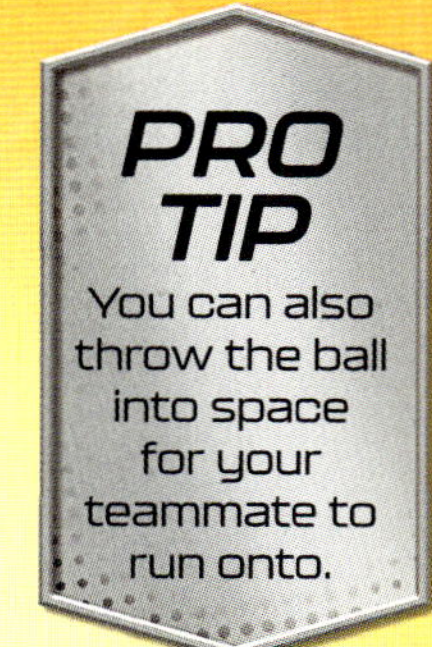

As you get better at throwing the ball, try aiming at different targets to improve your accuracy.

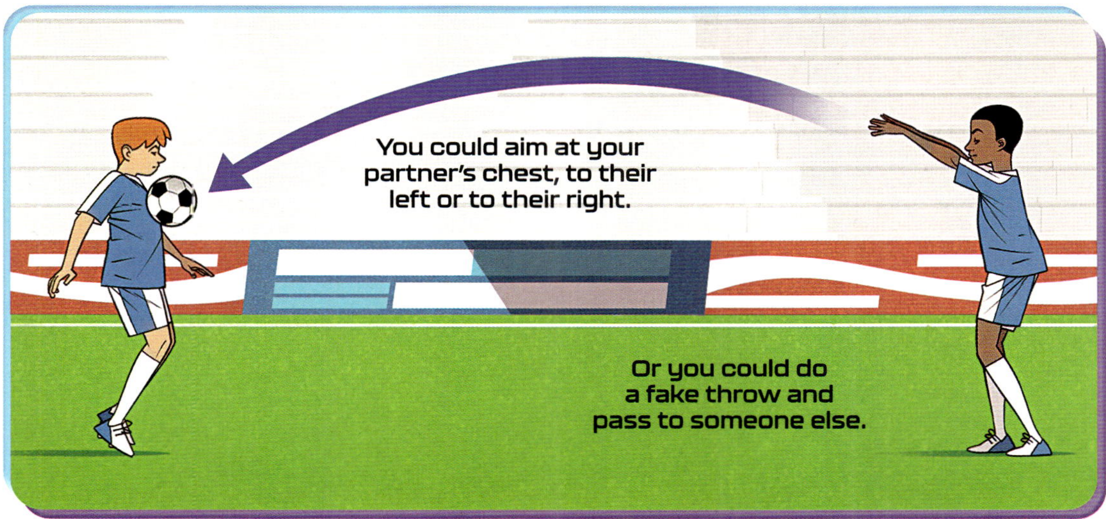

LONG THROW-INS

Some teams have a player who specializes in throwing the ball a long way. You can practice this technique to develop a long, accurate throw-in.

SKILL LEVEL

6 OUT OF **10**

1 TAKE A COUPLE OF QUICK STEPS FORWARD.

Judge your run-up to stop before the line.

2 PLANT YOUR FRONT FOOT JUST BEHIND THE LINE AND BRING THE BALL BACK.

Arch your back to throw the ball harder.

STARTING THE THROW WITH A WIDE STANCE CAN GIVE IT MORE MOMENTUM.

3 WHIP YOUR ARMS FORWARD TO CATAPULT THE BALL AWAY.

Make sure both feet stay on the ground.

FOUL THROWS

If you break one of the rules when taking a throw-in, the referee will give the throw-in to the other team. The pictures below show how you could end up throwing away possession.

FOUL THROW!

Your feet are fully over the line. They must be on or behind the line.

FOUL THROW!

One of your feet is off the ground as you throw. They must both be on the ground.

FOUL THROW!

The ball is too far forward. You must throw it from behind your head.

CORNER KICK

A corner is given when the ball comes off the defending team and crosses the line either side of the goal. You can pass short to a teammate, or cross long into the box.

WHERE TO STRIKE

Strike the ball off-center, so it spins as it travels through the air.

BENDING LEFT OR RIGHT

Place the ball so that the corner flag doesn't block your run-up. If you're right-footed, using the inside of your foot makes the ball bend to the left. If you're left-footed, it will bend to the right.

Here's how a left-footed player bends the ball away from the goal.

And here's how a right-footed player bends the ball toward the goal.

DRIVEN CORNER

SKILL LEVEL 8 OUT OF 10

When you swing a corner in, the ball moves more slowly because it's curving through the air. Sometimes driving the ball fast and straight can catch the other team off guard.

1 PLANT YOUR NON-KICKING FOOT AND KEEP YOUR HEAD OVER THE BALL.

2 WITH YOUR TOES POINTING DOWN, STRIKE BELOW THE CENTER OF THE BALL WITH YOUR INSTEP.

3 FOLLOW THROUGH TO SEND THE BALL HARD AND LOW INTO THE BOX.

CORNER MOVES

Here's how a driven corner can work. Aim for a teammate on the near side of the goal.

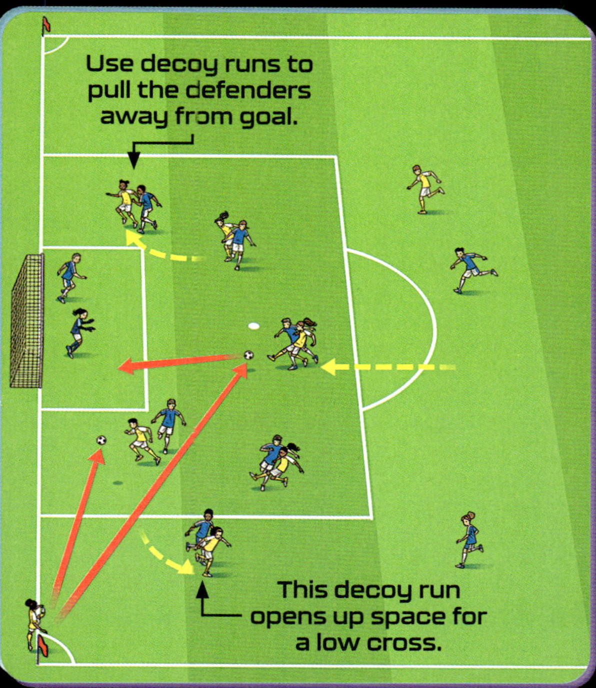

SIGNALLING THE MOVE

Signal what kind of cross you're about to do, so your teammates know where to move. Decide on the signals together in training, so the other team can't tell what they mean.

BENDING A FREE KICK

When you get a free kick near the other team's penalty area, your opponents will form a wall between the ball and the goal. To score, you need to get the ball past this wall of players.

SKILL LEVEL

8 OUT OF **10**

SPREAD YOUR ARMS FOR BALANCE.

AIM FOR THE CORNER OF THE GOAL.

CURL THE BALL TO MAKE IT MORE DIFFICULT FOR THE GOALIE TO JUDGE WHERE IT'S GOING.

LEAN BACK SLIGHTLY TO LIFT THE BALL OVER THE WALL.

FREE KICK PRACTICE

To bend a free kick, you'll need to use the swerve techniques on pages 36 to 39. Practice bending the ball in both directions, to keep the goalkeeper guessing.

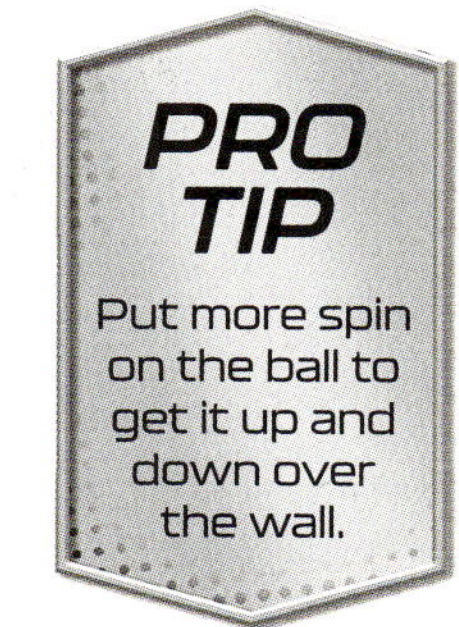

Use flag markers to help practice your swerve kicks.

The inside of your foot bends it one way.

The outside of your foot bends it the other way.

FREE KICK TRICKS

You don't have to shoot from a free kick. Try these tricks to surprise the other team and get past their defense.

BACK PASS SWITCH

SKILL LEVEL 6 OUT OF 10

YOUR TEAMMATE CAN NOW SHOOT.

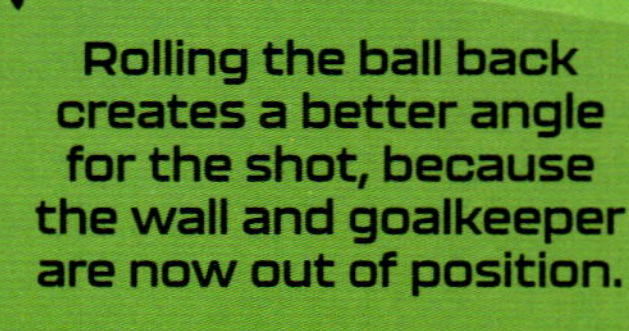

Rolling the ball back creates a better angle for the shot, because the wall and goalkeeper are now out of position.

DUMMY CROSS-OVERS

In this trick, one player does a "dummy run," then leaves the ball for another player to quickly swoop in and take the shot.

PRO TIP

A dummy run can also block the goalie's view of the real shot.

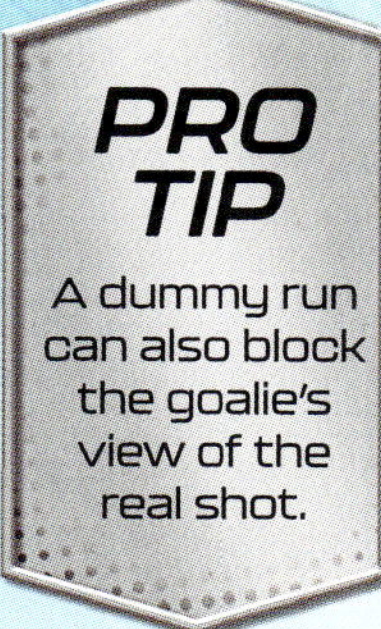

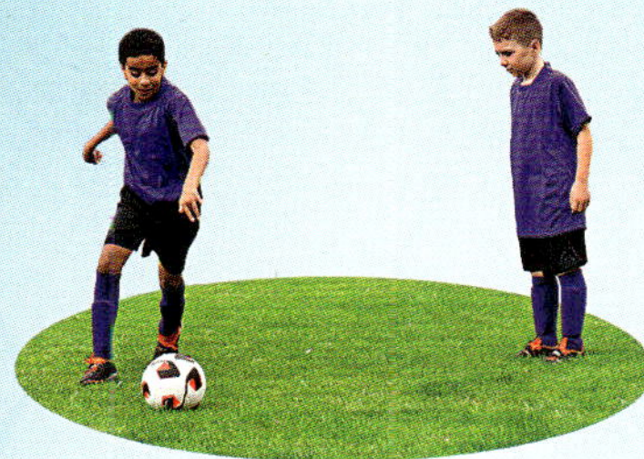

1 STAND AS IF YOUR TEAMMATE IS GOING TO SHOOT, NOT YOU.

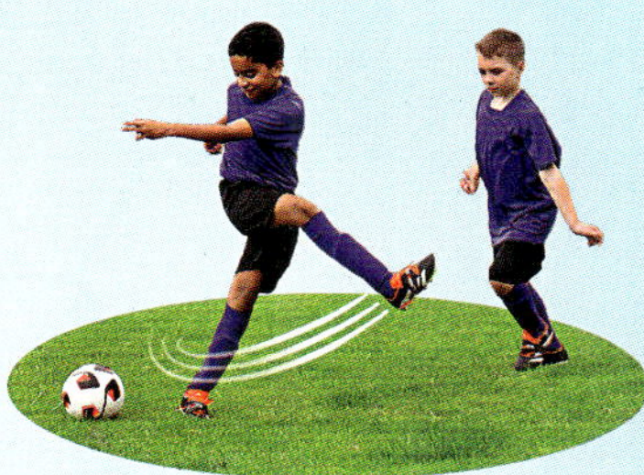

2 YOUR TEAMMATE STEPS OVER THE BALL AT THE LAST MOMENT.

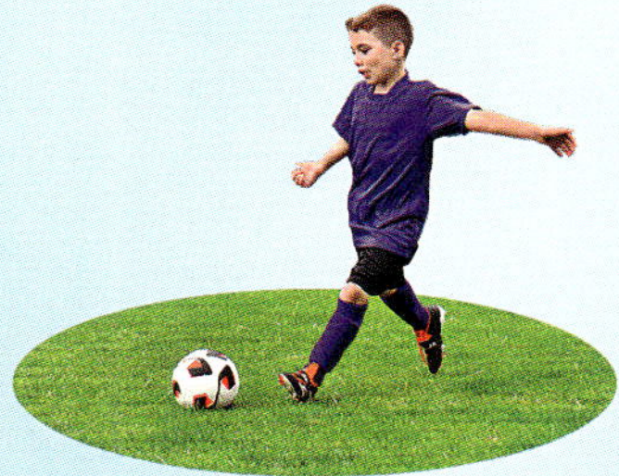

3 TIME YOUR RUN TO SHOOT JUST AFTER THEIR DUMMY SHOT.

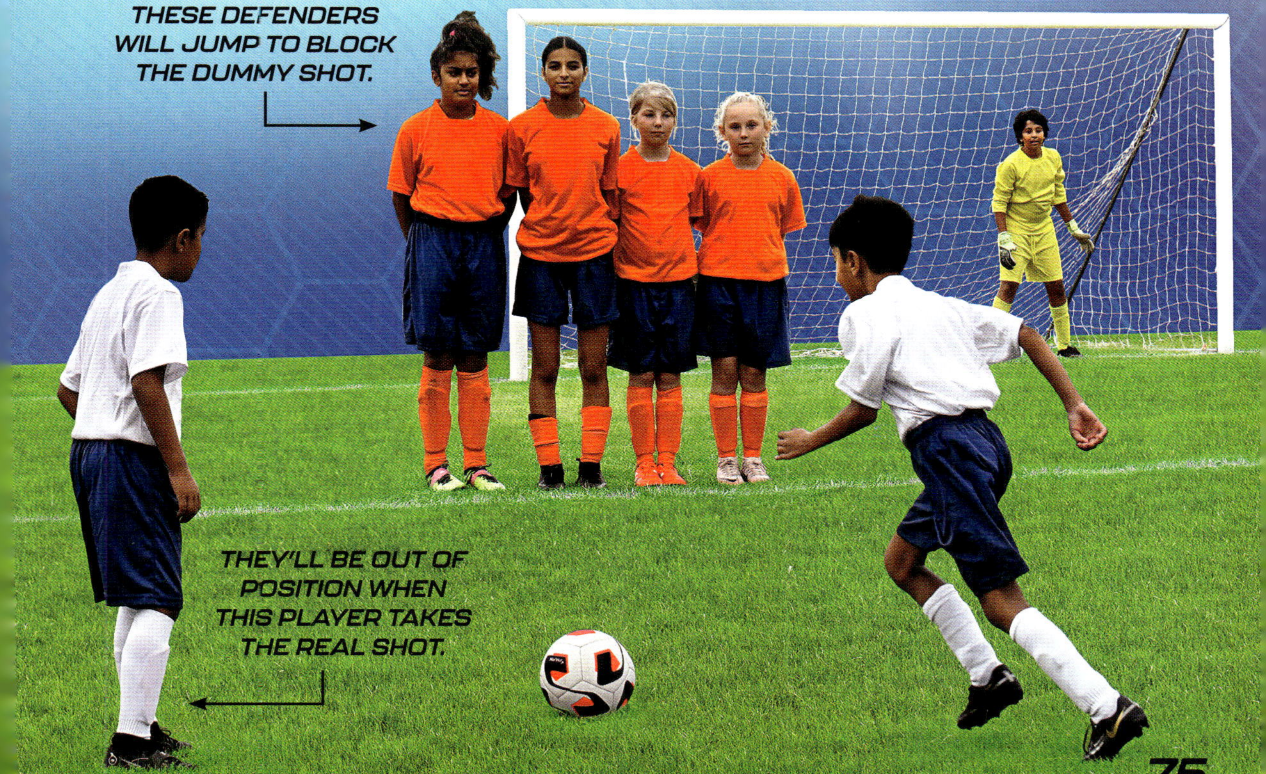

THESE DEFENDERS WILL JUMP TO BLOCK THE DUMMY SHOT.
THEY'LL BE OUT OF POSITION WHEN THIS PLAYER TAKES THE REAL SHOT.

PENALTIES

To score a penalty, you need both skill to beat the goalie and mental strength to stay calm under pressure. Work on your aim so you can send the ball exactly where you want it to go.

SKILL LEVEL

7 OUT OF **10**

1 PLACE THE BALL ON THE PENALTY SPOT, WAIT FOR THE WHISTLE, THEN RUN UP TO SHOOT.

2 FOR A FIRM, ACCURATE SHOT, STRIKE THE BALL USING THE INSIDE OF YOUR FOOT.

3 KEEP YOUR EYES ON THE BALL AND FOLLOW THROUGH.

PRO TIP

Block out the noise and try to stay focussed while you wait to take your kick.

FOR A MORE POWERFUL SHOT, POINT YOUR TOES DOWN AND DRIVE THROUGH WITH YOUR INSTEP (SEE PAGE 48).

TACTICS

A powerful shot into the corner is almost impossible to save. You can also score by tricking the goalkeeper into diving the wrong way.

If you're going for power, pick your spot before you run up, but try not to make it obvious.

Then strike the ball with everything you've got!

To trick the goalie, line up to shoot one way, then whip the ball into the opposite corner.

You could slow down just before you shoot, to see which way the goalie dives. Then roll the ball the other way.

GOALKEEPER TIPS

- Try to find out about the other team's penalty taker. Do they usually shoot left or right, high or low?
- Stay on the goal line until the ball is kicked.
- Try putting the penalty taker off by staring them in the eye, or spreading your arms wide to make yourself look bigger.

GOALKEEPER'S STANCE

If you're a goalie, you need to be alert and ready to act quickly. When the other team is nearing your goal, set yourself to spring into action.

SKILL LEVEL

2 OUT OF **10**

WATCH THE ATTACKER CLOSELY FOR CLUES THEY'RE ABOUT TO SHOOT.

LEAN FORWARD SLIGHTLY AND BEND YOUR KNEES.

HAVE YOUR HANDS READY, AT ROUGHLY WAIST HEIGHT.

KEEP YOUR WEIGHT BALANCED SO YOU CAN DIVE TO EITHER SIDE.

SHIFT YOUR WEIGHT TO THE BALLS OF YOUR FEET.

CATCHING THE BALL

For high balls into the box, the best catching technique is the W shape.

The palms of your hands face outward and your index fingers and thumbs form a "W" around the back of the ball.

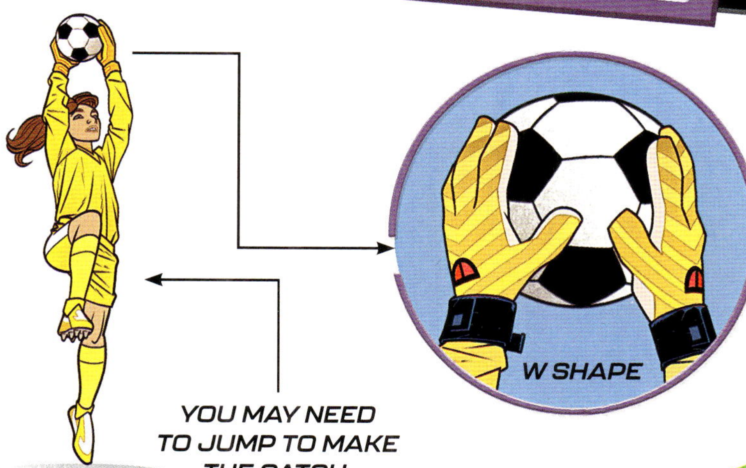

(See page 90 for more on high catches.)

CATCHING PRACTICE

Practice catching shots while keeping on the move.

Lay out a zigzag pattern of markers, 6ft (2m) apart.

Weave through the markers, staying in your stance.

A teammate chips the ball towards you.

Throw the ball back so they can take another shot.

SHOT STOPPING

The best position for stopping a shot depends on how high and fast it is. Here are some options.

SCOOPING

Scooping, or cradling, is the safest way to catch a ball at waist or stomach height.

SKILL LEVEL

5 OUT OF **10**

LEAN INTO THE SHOT SO YOU'RE NOT KNOCKED OFF BALANCE.

1 ANGLE YOUR ARMS DOWNWARD TO LET THE BALL ROLL INTO YOUR CHEST.

JUMP TO GET YOUR CHEST BEHIND HIGHER SHOTS.

2 WRAP YOUR HANDS AROUND THE BALL, CLUTCHING IT TO YOUR CHEST.

THE BENDING SCOOP

For balls along the ground, bend down and scoop them into your hands.

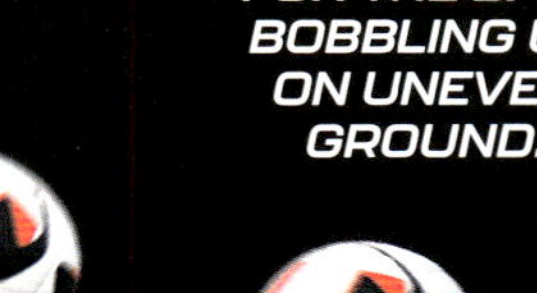

BARRIER POSITION

If you have time to get your knee to the ground, you can create an extra barrier with your leg. This is also known as a "K save."

PRO TIP

Cup your hands around the ball and quickly lift it away from attackers.

COLLAPSING SAVE

If you don't have time to move in line with the ball and scoop it up, it's best to "collapse" behind it.

1 STEP TO THE SIDE AND LET YOUR KNEES COLLAPSE UNDER YOU.

2 GET YOUR BODY BEHIND THE BALL AND WRAP YOUR HANDS AROUND IT.

3 BRING YOUR KNEES UP TO PROTECT YOURSELF IN A CROWDED GOAL AREA.

KEEP YOUR HANDS AND ARMS FREE TO GRAB THE BALL.

COLLAPSING PRACTICE

Mark out a smaller goal size for your teammate to aim at and try to save their shots with your hands.

COLLAPSING SAVE TIPS

- Get down to the ground as quickly as possible.
- Avoid doing acrobatic leaps that might let the ball through.
- Use your hands to stop the ball squeezing under you.

DIVING SAVE

SKILL LEVEL 8 OUT OF 10

You'll often have to dive to reach a well struck shot. Keep your eyes on the ball all the way.

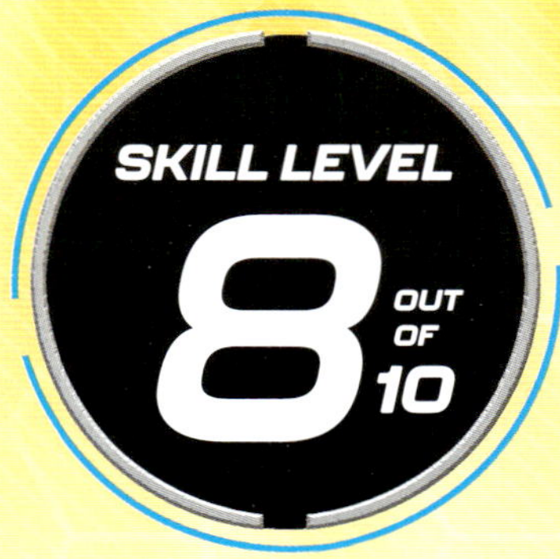

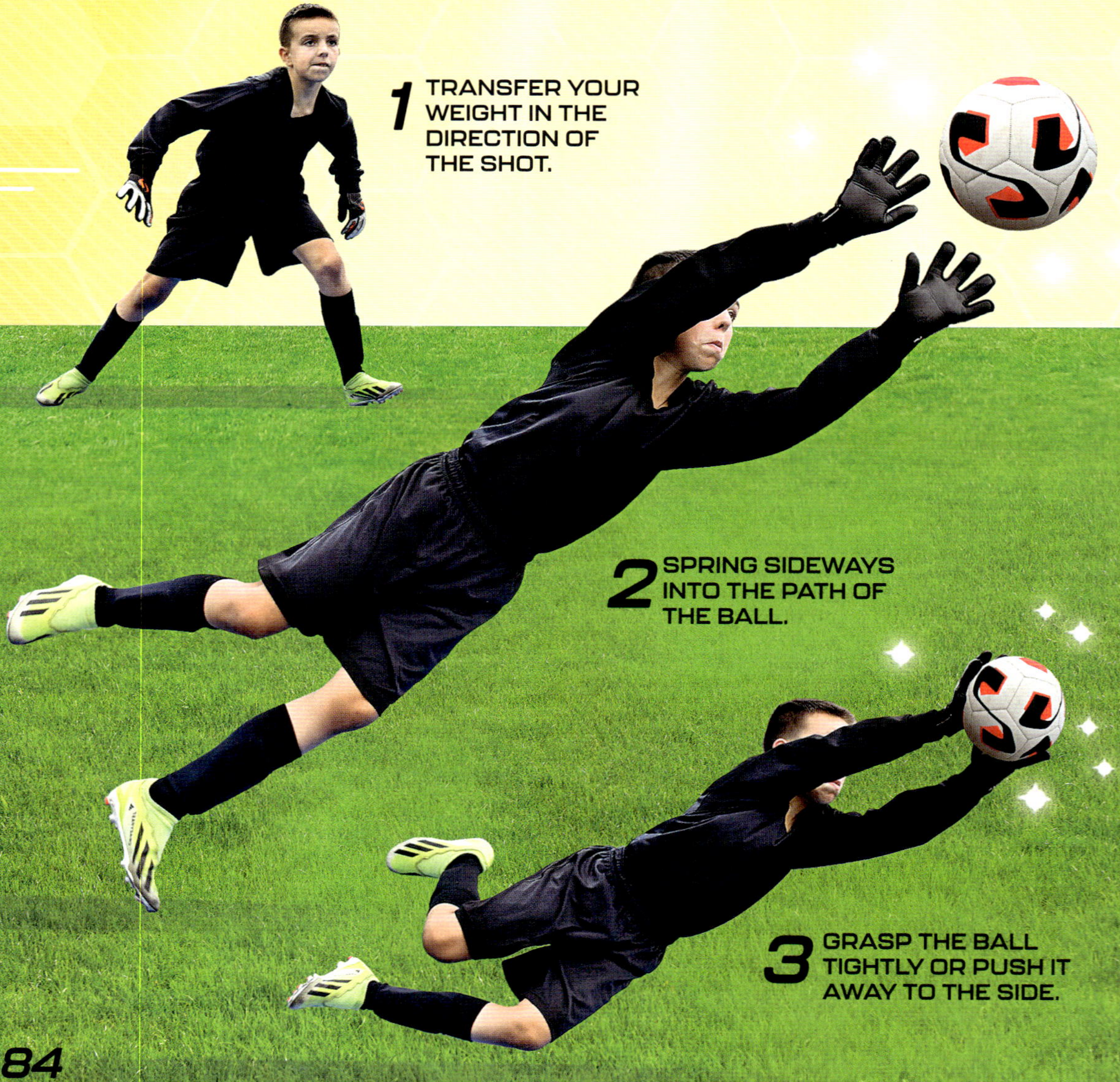

1 TRANSFER YOUR WEIGHT IN THE DIRECTION OF THE SHOT.

2 SPRING SIDEWAYS INTO THE PATH OF THE BALL.

3 GRASP THE BALL TIGHTLY OR PUSH IT AWAY TO THE SIDE.

DIVING SAVE DRILLS

Here are two ways to practice diving – falling to one side and twisting around.

FALLING TO ONE SIDE

TWISTING AROUND

NARROWING THE ANGLE

If you stay back, an attacker has more of the goal to aim at.

Here, the attacker has a clear view of goal.

By moving forward, you narrow the attacker's shooting angles, and make it easier to save their shot.

Now, the attacker has a smaller target area to aim at.

KEEP ON YOUR TOES, READY TO SPRING INTO ACTION.

ALTERNATING ANGLES

Practice coming forward to narrow the angles by asking two teammates to stand on either side of the penalty area.

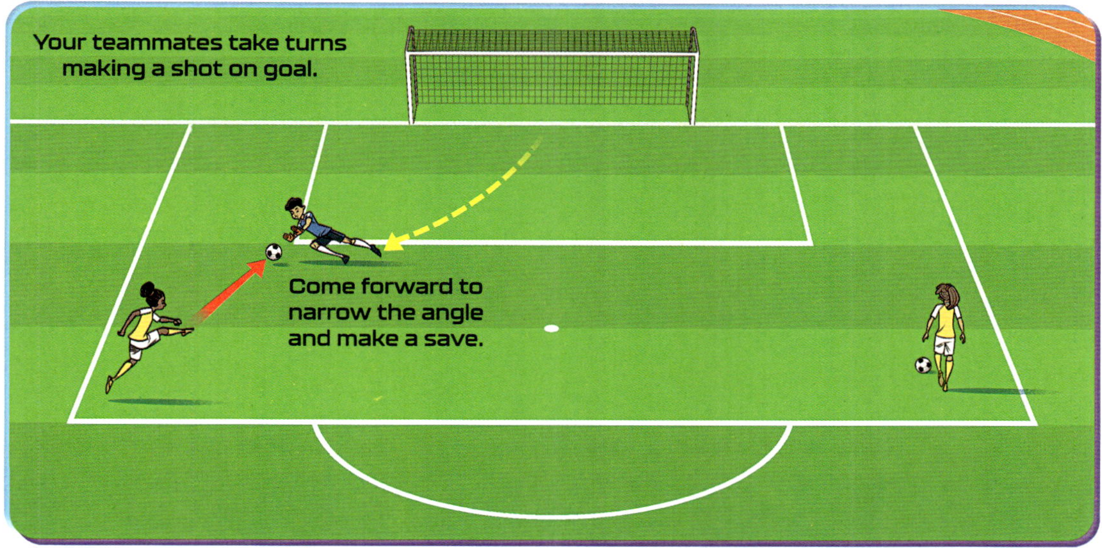

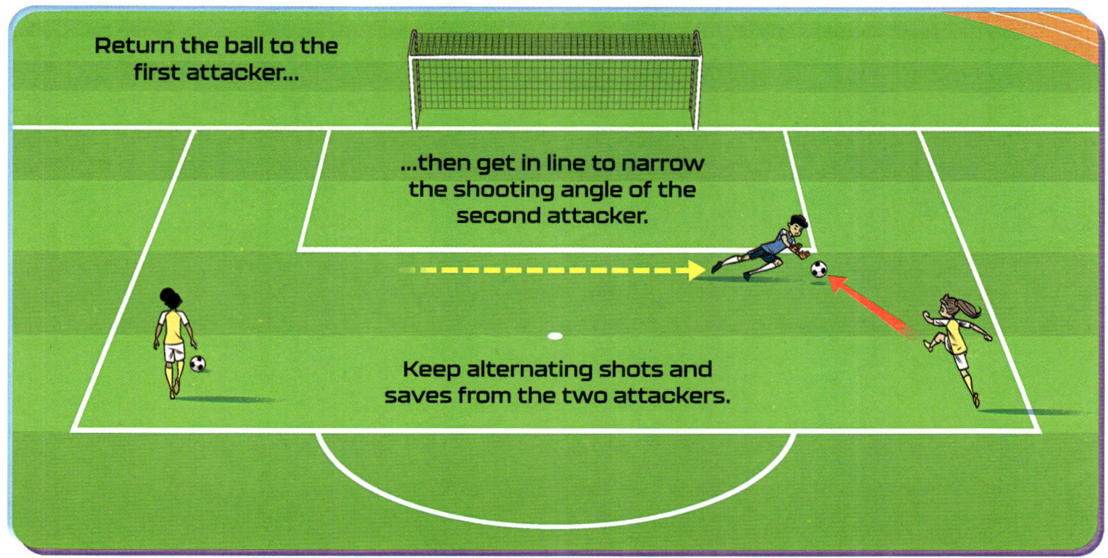

ONE-ON-ONES

SKILL LEVEL 7 OUT OF 10

When there are no defenders to help you out, rush forward to block the attacker's route to goal.

1 WATCH FOR THE BALL COMING THROUGH AND RUN FORWARD.

2 SLOW DOWN ONCE THE ATTACKER HAS THE BALL.

3 STAY ON YOUR FEET AND TRY TO FORCE THEM WIDE.

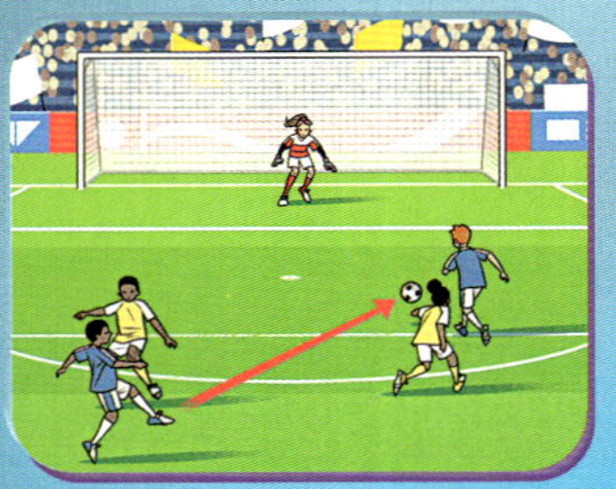

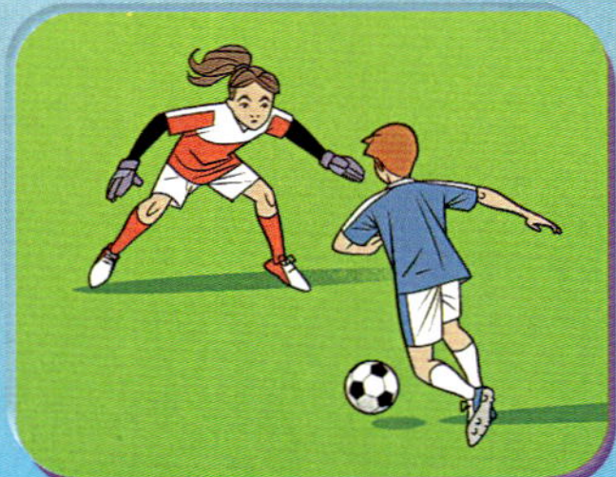

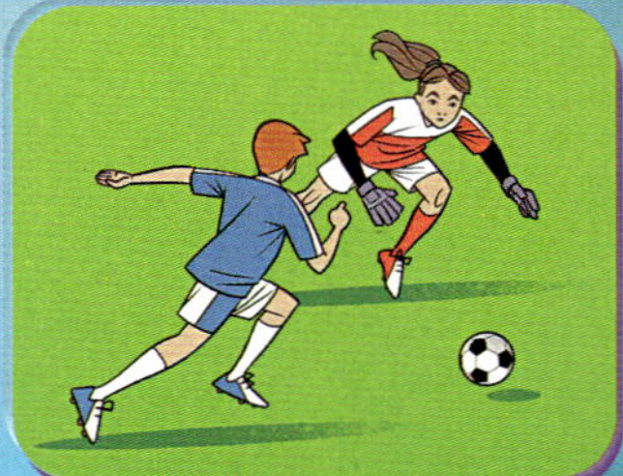

If the player tries to shoot, quickly make yourself as big as possible.

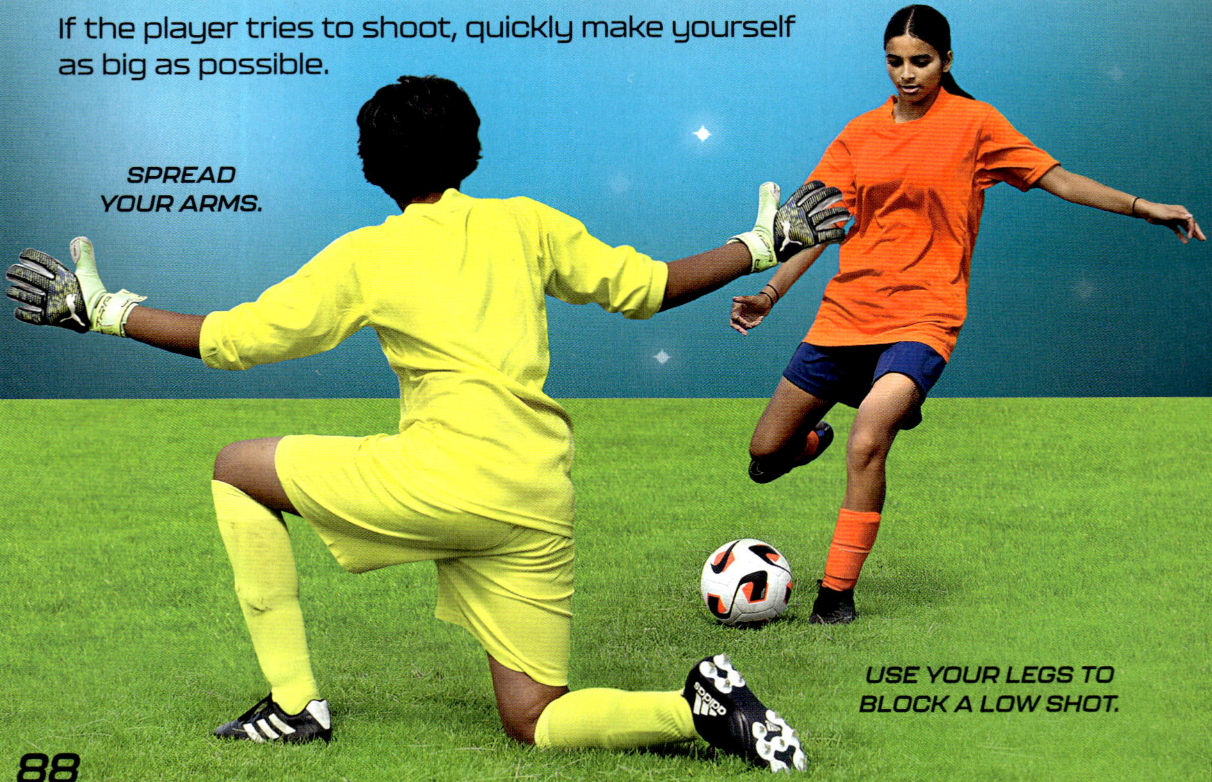
SPREAD YOUR ARMS.
USE YOUR LEGS TO BLOCK A LOW SHOT.

DIVING AT THEIR FEET

When an attacker attempts to dribble around you, one option is to dive at their feet. Only do this if you feel confident you'll win the ball.

TRY TO GRAB THE BALL OR PUSH IT AWAY FROM THE ATTACKER.

KEEP YOUR FACE AWAY FROM THE PLAYER'S FEET.

FOUL!

Be sure to make contact with the ball first. If you catch the player first, it's a foul. If the foul happens inside the box, the referee will award a penalty kick.

WRAP YOUR BODY AROUND THE BALL FOR EXTRA PROTECTION.

DEALING WITH CROSSES

Be ready to defend high crosses by catching the ball or punching it away.

BEAT OPPONENTS TO THE BALL BY CATCHING IT ABOVE THEIR HEADS. (THEY CAN'T USE THEIR HANDS!)

SKILL LEVEL

7 OUT OF **10**

GOALIE'S BALL!

SHOUT FOR THE BALL SO YOUR DEFENDERS KNOW TO LEAVE IT TO YOU.

QUICKLINKS
Catch or punch? Discover how to handle crosses like a pro.
Usborne.com/Quicklinks

LIFT THE LEG NEAREST TO THE ATTACKERS TO PROTECT YOUR BODY AGAINST CHALLENGES.

JUMP OFF ONE LEG TO CATCH THE BALL.

PUNCHING CROSSES

If a clean catch isn't possible, try punching the ball away instead.

PRO TIP

Punch the ball firmly with the flat area between your knuckles and finger joints.

TO GET MAXIMUM POWER, USE BOTH FISTS TOGETHER.

YOU MAY HAVE TO STRETCH FOR THE BALL WITH ONE HAND.

TRY TO BEAT ANY ONCOMING OPPONENTS TO THE BALL.

TAKE A RUNNING JUMP.

TIPPING THE BALL

Some shots are too high to catch, but even just getting your fingertips onto the ball can be enough to prevent a goal.

KEEP YOUR WRIST AND FINGERS STIFF TO STOP THE BALL.

SKILL LEVEL

7 OUT OF **10**

TRY TO TIP THE BALL OVER THE BAR OR AROUND THE POST.

LAUNCH YOURSELF IN THE DIRECTION OF THE BALL.

QUICKLINKS
Watch videos of some amazing fingertip saves, and learn some extra tips.
usborne.com/Quicklinks

HAND POSITION

Keep your palm open and your fingers spread wide.

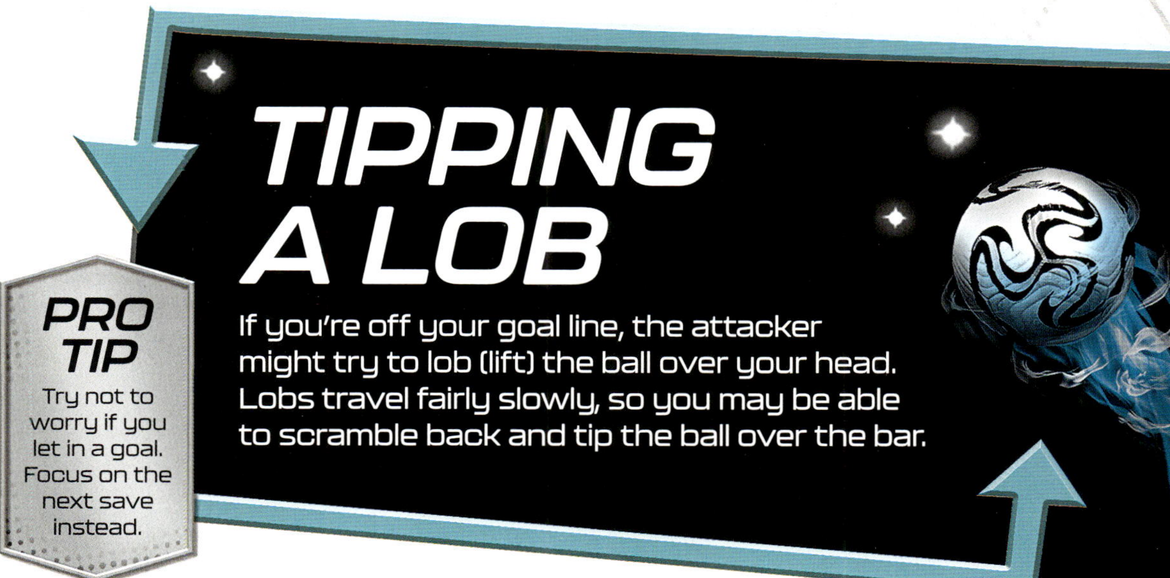

TIPPING A LOB

If you're off your goal line, the attacker might try to lob (lift) the ball over your head. Lobs travel fairly slowly, so you may be able to scramble back and tip the ball over the bar.

Try this drill with a partner, to practice getting back in position.

BEING A TEAM

Soccer is a team sport. To do well, you need to work together and support each other, both on and off the field.

EVERY PLAYER IS IMPORTANT. YOU WIN TOGETHER AND YOU LOSE TOGETHER.

LISTEN TO YOUR MANAGER OR COACH.

THEY'LL HELP YOU IMPROVE AS A TEAM.

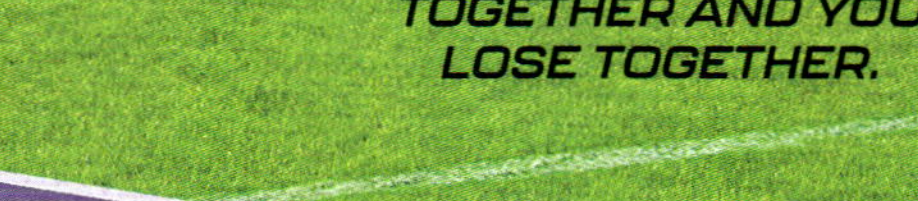

The team captains lead their teams when they're on the field and work with the referee to help the game go smoothly.

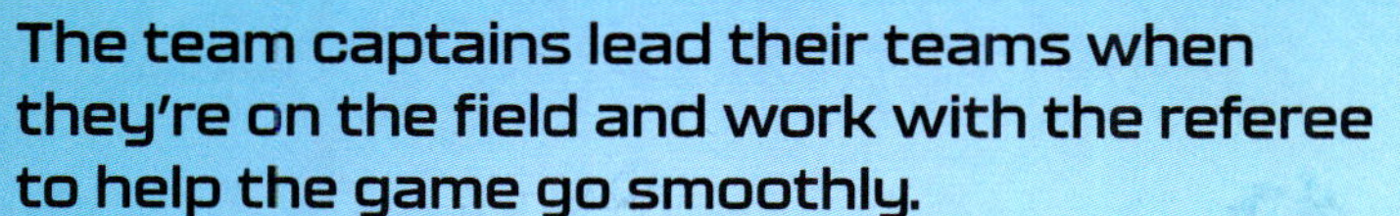

Celebrating a win is easier than handling a loss, but you'll have to learn to do both!

BE THERE FOR YOUR TEAMMATES WHEN THEY NEED YOU.

IN A GAME

Parents and carers can play a key role too, being positive and supporting the whole team.

THE RULES

The rules for soccer are known as the laws of the game. By following the rules, players all over the world can enjoy the same game.

THE REF

QUICKLINKS
You can look up all the laws of the game in the FA Handbook.

usborne.com/Quicklinks

The laws are enforced on the field by the referee. Referees can stop play by blowing their whistle, and have the power to show yellow or red cards.

A YELLOW CARD IS A WARNING.

If a player gets two yellow cards in the same game, it converts to a red card.

A RED CARD IS A SENDING-OFF.

The player must leave the field for the rest of the game, and can't be replaced.

THE REF POINTS TO THE PENALTY SPOT TO SIGNAL A PENALTY.

VAR

In some televised games, a Video Assistant Referee (VAR) might use video technology to help make decisions. If the referee isn't sure, VAR can offer a second opinion.

FREE KICKS

If a player does something that breaks the rules, the other side gets a free kick. There are two types of free kicks, direct and indirect.

DIRECT

You can score directly from a direct free kick. If it's awarded in the penalty area, it's a penalty.

Reasons for awarding a direct free kick include:
- handball
- kicks, trips or pushes
- holding or barging an opponent
- biting or spitting at someone

INDIRECT

You're not allowed to score directly from an indirect free kick. The ball has to touch another player first.

Reasons for awarding an indirect free kick include:
- obstructing an opponent
- preventing the goalkeeper from releasing the ball
- a player being offside

OFFSIDE

Offside is when a player in the opponent's half is beyond the last defender when the ball is played, then goes on to touch the ball or get involved with play in some way. The assistant referee signals "offside" by raising their flag.

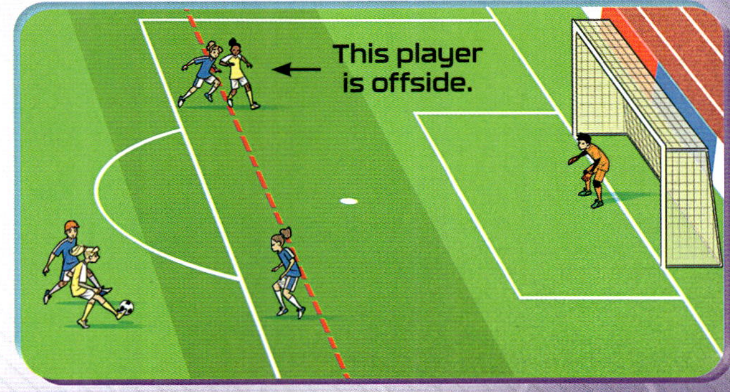

RESPECT

Everyone has the right to play, watch and enjoy soccer. As well as following the rules, it's important to show each other respect. No one should feel picked on or left out.

IN A GAME

If an opponent is down with an injury, you can kick the ball out of play. This creates time to check if the player is OK.

WARNING

Players who don't show respect will be asked to apologize. For serious offenses, they could be sent off and suspended by their club.

AFTER A TACKLE, PLAYERS OFTEN HELP EACH OTHER UP TO SHOW NO HARD FEELINGS.

CODE OF CONDUCT

Players at all levels are encouraged to sign a code of conduct, agreeing to behave in a certain way. Here's an example:

When playing soccer, I will:

- Always play to the best of my ability
- Play fairly – I won't cheat, dive, complain or waste time
- Respect my teammates, the other team, the referee and my coach
- Play by the rules, as directed by the referee
- Shake hands with the other team and referee before or at the end of the game
- Listen and respond to what my coach tells me
- Understand that a coach has to do what is best for the team and not one individual player
- Talk to someone I trust or the club welfare officer if I'm unhappy about anything at my club

There's also a recommended code of conduct for parents, carers and fans:

- Remember that children play for FUN
- Applaud effort and good play as well as success
- Always respect the game officials' decisions
- Remain outside the field of play and within the Designated Spectators' Area (where provided)
- Let the coach do their job and don't confuse the players by interfering
- Encourage the players to respect the opposition, referee and game officials
- Support positively. When players make a mistake, offer them encouragement not criticism
- Never engage in, or tolerate, offensive, insulting, or abusive language or behavior

SHOW RACISM THE RED CARD

Show Racism the Red Card is an anti-racism education charity that was founded in the UK around 30 years ago. Red Card uses the high-profile status of soccer and soccer players to help tackle racism in society.

The charity was founded in the 1990s, inspired by soccer player Shaka Hislop's own experience.

When Shaka was filling his car with gas one evening, a group of local soccer fans started shouting racial abuse at him.

As they got closer, they recognized who it was and their tone changed instantly. They didn't want to insult their team's star goalkeeper – they wanted his autograph!

"THAT'S WHEN I REALIZED I COULD HARNESS MY INFLUENCE AS A PROFESSIONAL SOCCER PLAYER TO MAKE A DIFFERENCE."
SHAKA HISLOP

Shaka turned his negative experience into a positive one. He started visiting schools with his teammates to challenge racism through education.

Now Show Racism the Red Card delivers sessions to over 50,000 people a year, from children in schools to adults in their workplace to events in soccer stadiums.

BREAKING DOWN BARRIERS

There are many more opportunities for women and girls to play soccer today, but it's not always easy.

The expert adviser on this book, Naomi Bedeau, faced many challenges on her way to becoming a professional soccer player. Here's just one example...

In the park one day, two boys took turns picking players for their teams. Naomi was the only girl there and the last to be picked. When the game began, no one passed to her.

Eventually she intercepted the ball and let her soccer skills do the talking. Only then did the boys' attitudes to her change, and she was finally included.

> *"MY BROTHER GOT PICKED BEFORE ME, AND I'M MUCH BETTER AT SOCCER THAN HIM!"*
> *NAOMI BEDEAU*

In 2025, Naomi was selected to represent Grenada in the World Cup Qualifiers.

The young soccer players in this book are from Oadby Owls FC in Leicestershire, UK.

The club is for girls and boys of all abilities, from the age of three. Its aim is to give everyone the opportunity to enjoy soccer in a safe and friendly environment.

> *"I AM IMMENSELY PROUD OF THE CHILDREN WHO HAVE PARTICIPATED IN THIS AMAZING INITIATIVE. INCLUSIVITY AND A SENSE OF BELONGING ARE EXTREMELY IMPORTANT IN THIS EVER-CHANGING WORLD. EVERYONE SHOULD FEEL VALUED, APPRECIATED AND RESPECTED."*
> *HAF KATIB, CHAIRPERSON OF OADBY OWLS FC*

GLOSSARY

Here are some of the key soccer words, and what they mean.

Clearance – when the ball is kicked or headed away from goal

Coach – a person who runs training sessions

Corner kick – a set play for the attacking team that's taken next to the corner flag

Cross – a sideways pass into the opposition's box from near the touchline

Dribble – run with the ball at your feet

Drill – a training routine

Feint – a trick where you pretend to dribble one way, then go the other. Or pretend to shoot and then don't.

Foul – something that's against the rules, e.g. a dangerous tackle

Free kick – a set play given when the other team commits a foul

Goal kick – a set play for the defending team when the ball comes off an attacker and goes wide of goal

Goal line – the line from one corner flag to the other, marking the end of the field

Instep – the top of your foot

Intercept – win possession by blocking an opponent's pass

Jockey – block your opponent's route to goal without tackling them

Juggling – keeping the ball in the air without using your hands

Manager – the person who picks the players and the formation. Sometimes called the head coach.

Offside – a foul conceded when you play the ball forward in the opposition half, but one of your teammates in the attack is closer to the goal than the last defender

One-on-one – when you're through on goal with just the goalie to beat

One-two – a quick pass to a teammate that lets you run past your opponent and collect the return pass

Penalty – a free kick for the attacking team that's taken from the penalty spot. All players except the taker and the goalie must stand outside the area.

Possession – when one team has control of the ball

Rebound – a loose ball that's bounced off the goalie back into the penalty area

Referee – the person on the field who makes sure both teams play by the rules

Set play – a pass or shot where the ball is put back into play after a stoppage, e.g. a free kick or throw-in

Shielding – stopping the opponent from getting to the ball by putting your body in the way

Tackle – a challenge on the opponent when they have the ball

Throw-in – a set play taken from the touchline where you throw the ball to a teammate

Touchline – the line from one goal line to the other, marking the side of the field

Volley – a shot or pass when the ball is in the air

Wall – a line of defenders between the ball and the goal when a free kick is taken

CREDITS

Cover design by Marc Maynard
Additional contributors: Gong Studios, Gill Harvey, Jonathan Sheikh-Miller, Richard Dungworth, Clive Gifford and Rob Lloyd Jones
Additional photo credits: Newcastle United FC (p100 top), Fulham Primary School (p100 bottom), Oxford United FC (p101 top), Chris Bunce Studio (p101 bottom)